V I S I O N S

VOLUME 3

FOR SENTIENT BEINGS WITH THE AFFLICTIONS
IS THE IMPURE VISION.
FOR THE MEDITATOR WITH TRANSIC ABSORPTION
IS THE VISION OF EXPERIENCE.
FOR THE ORNAMENTAL WHEEL OF THE SUGATA'S
INEXHAUSTIBLE BODY, VOICE AND MIND
IS THE PURE VISION.

MAHASIDDHA VIRUPA

VISIONS

VOLUME 3

The Life of the Buddha
Peter Della Santina

The Buddha Nature
The Five Paths to Enlightenment
The Ten Bhumis to Enlightenment
The Qualities of the Buddha
Khenpo Appey Rinpoche

The Gift of Dharma to Kublai Khan
Choegyal Phagpa

Buddhist Tantra: Some Introductory Remarks
His Holiness Sakya Trizin

The Song Given to Yeshe Dorje
The Instruction on Parting from the Four Attachments
The Verse Instruction on How to Guide Students to the Path and Result
Jetsun Rinpoche Dragpa Gyaltsen

Compiled and edited by
Acharya Migmar Tseten

Manjushri Press
Boston
2000

MANJUSHRI PRESS
P.O. BOX 391042
CAMBRIDGE, MA
02139 U.S.A.

Printed in Canada

ISBN 1-928709-02-8

10   9   8   7   6   5   4   3   2   1

Library of Congress Catalog card number 00-093673

DEDICATED TO THE GREAT TIBETAN YOGIS

JETSUN RINPOCHE DRAGPA GYALTSEN
AND JETSUN RINPOCHE MILAREPA:

MAY YOU SHOWER THE BLESSING OF SADDHADHARMA ON
ALL PRACTITIONERS, THAT THEY MAY ABANDON THE EIGHT
LOKADHARMA.

Contents

INTRODUCTION

In *The Life of the Buddha*, Peter Della Santina describes how the values of renunciation, love and compassion, and wisdom are illustrated by various episodes in the life of the Buddha and how we can look at his life as a lesson on how to achieve Enlightenment. By cultivating these three values, the Buddhist practitioner is able to remove the afflictions of attachment, aversion and ignorance and attain Enlightenment.

The Buddha Nature is a teaching given by Khenpo Appey Rinpoche and translated by Ngawang Samten. Rinpoche defines "Buddha nature" and explains the different signs of and obstacles to awakening Buddha nature. He also discusses the differences between the teachings of the Mind Only school and the Madhyamika school with respect to Buddha nature.

The Five Paths to Enlightenment is a second teaching given by Khenpo Appey Rinpoche and translated by Ngawang Samten. Rinpoche describes in detail the paths of accumulation, application, seeing, meditation and no more learning and discusses the differences between the Hinayana and Mahayana traditions.

The Ten Bhumis to Enlightenment is a third teaching given by Khenpo Appey Rinpoche and translated by Ngawang Samten. Rinpoche defines the term "bhumi" and describes in detail each of the ten Mahayana bhumis: the very joyful, the stainless, the issuing of light rays, the making of light rays, the purification of difficulties, direct manifestation, going to a far distance, the unshakeable, good intelligence and the cloud of dharma.

The Qualities of the Buddha is a fourth teaching given by Khenpo Appey Rinpoche and translated by Ngawang Samten. In this teaching, Rinpoche defines the term "Buddha" and explains in detail the qualities of the Buddha, starting with the qualities of the three bodies of Dharmakaya, Sambhogakaya and Nirmanakaya. Rinpoche explains these and the other special qualities of the Buddha, both according to Maitreya and Sakya Pandita.

The Gift of Dharma to Kublai Khan is a teaching given by Choegyal Phagpa, the fifth founding master of the Sakya tradition, to the Mongolian king Kublai Khan. The teaching was translated by Acharya Lobsang Jamspal and Acharya Manjusiddhartha.

Buddhist Tantra: Some Introductory Remarks is a teaching given by His Holiness Sakya Trizin. His Holiness begins the teaching by clarifying some misconceptions about Buddhist tantra and then defines the different meanings of the word "tantra." He then explains that tantra was taught by the Lord Buddha as part of the Mahayana Vehicle, which consists of the Paramitayana, the Perfection Vehicle, which is also known as the Cause Vehicle, and the Mantrayana, the Tantric (or Mantra) Vehicle, which is also known as the "Result Vehicle." His Holiness explains the differences between these two vehicles and explains why the Tantric Vehicle is superior to the Perfection Vehicle. His Holiness emphasizes the importance of the Guru and the lineage transmission as prerequisites for the practice of tantra, which should only be practised by a qualified disciple. His Holiness concludes by pointing out the differences and similarities between the general Mahayana and the Vajrayana and between Buddhist Tantra and Hindu Tantra.

The following three songs were composed by Jetsun Dragpa Gyaltsen and translated from Tibetan into English by Acharya Migmar Tseten and Kunga Namdol.

The Song Given to Yeshe Dorje describes the nine "limbs" of the Guru, abhisheka, samaya, hearing, upadesha, diligence, place, conducive circumstances, and dharma friends, each of which is a necessary condition to practicing the path. The complete realization of three additional limbs, wisdom, method and conduct, is the necessary condition to achieving Buddhahood. Thus, Buddhahood is achieved through these twelve limbs.

The Instruction on Parting from the Four Attachments is a teaching based on the classic Sakyapa mind training of Freedom from the Four Attachments. It begins with meditations on the four common foundations, the preciousness of human birth, impermanence and death, the faults of samsara, and karma. These meditations gradually lead to the meditations on loving kindness, compassion and exchanging self and others. The teaching concludes with instructions on abandoning the extremes and the gradually development of the right view of non-duality and inexpressibility by practicing calm abiding and insight meditation.

The Verse Instruction on How to Guide Students to the Path and Result is based on the graduated meditations of the Lamdre teachings. It starts with meditations on the faults of samsara, taking refuge, the two Bodhicittas, and impermanence. Then, those with greater intelligence are led into Vajrayana Abhisheka and trained gradually in the meditation on the perfect view, the generation stage, the three preliminaries and the completion stage practices.

PUBLISHER'S ACKNOWLEDGEMENT

We want to acknowledge the invaluable contributions of Jetsun Rinpoche Dragpa Gyaltsen, Choegyal Phagpa, His Holiness Sakya Trizin, Khenpo Appey Rinpoche, Tulku Thondup Rinpoche, and Peter Della Santina and express our deep respect, appreciation and gratitude to them.

The generosity of an anonymous benefactor has made the publication of this edition of *Visions* possible. We rejoice and thank our benefactor for the support. Lastly, we thank all those who contributed their skills to produce this issue. We pray for their well-being

May this publication benefit all living beings.

THE LIFE OF THE BUDDHA

By Peter Della Santina

There are three values of paramount importance that emerge from the life of the Buddha: (1) renunciation, (2) love and compassion, and (3) wisdom. These values stand out very clearly in many episodes throughout his life. It is no coincidence that these three, taken together, are the essential requisites for the attainment of nirvana, or enlightenment. According to the teaching of Buddhism, there are three afflictions which cause us to be reborn again and again in the wilderness of cyclical existence—namely, attachment, aversion, and ignorance. These afflictions are eliminated by the correctives of renunciation, love and compassion, and wisdom, respectively. Through cultivating these three attitudes, the Buddhist practitioner is able to remove the afflictions and attain enlightenment. Consequently, it is no accident that these attitudes should feature so prominently in the life of the Buddha Shakyamuni.

Let us consider these essential attitudes one by one, beginning with renunciation. As in the case of love and compassion, the first signs of renunciation manifested themselves very early in the life of the Buddha. Basically, renunciation is the recognition that all existence is permeated by suffering. When you realize this, it leads to what we might call a turning about, that is to say, the realization that all of common life is permeated by suffering causes us to look for something more or something different. This is precisely why suffering is counted as the first of the Four Noble Truths, and why the clear recognition of the reality and universality of suffering is the essence of renunciation.

Now, as it happens, Prince Siddhartha is believed to have participated, as we might expect, in the annual plowing ceremony of his clan at the tender age of seven. It was then that, while watching the proceedings, the young prince noticed a worm that had been unearthed being devoured by a bird. This casual observation led Siddhartha to contemplate the realities of life—to recognize the inescapable fact that all living beings kill one another to survive, and that this is a great source of suffering. Already, at this early age, we find in the Buddha's biography the beginning of the recognition that life as we know it is permeated by suffering.

If we look again at the biographical accounts of Siddhartha's early life, we soon come to the famous episode of the four sights that moved him to renounce the life of a householder and adopt the life of an ascetic in order to seek the truth. Seeing an old man, a sick man, and a corpse led him to consider why it was that he should feel unsettled by these sights. Clearly, he himself was not immune to these conditions but was subject to the inevitable succession of old age, sickness, and death. This recognition led the prince to develop a sense of detachment from the ephemeral pleasures of this world and prompted him to seek the ultimate truth about existence by way of renunciation.

It is important to remember at this stage that the prince's renunciation was not prompted by despair occurring in the ordinary course of life. He enjoyed the greatest possible happiness and privilege known in his day, and yet he recognized the suffering inherent in sentient existence and realized that, no matter how much we may indulge ourselves in pleasures of the senses, eventually we must face the realities of old age, sickness, and death. Understanding this—and encouraged by the fourth sight, that of an ascetic— Siddhartha was moved to renounce the life of a householder and to seek ultimate truth for the benefit of all living beings.

Let us look next at the attitude of love and compassion, which also appears very early in the life of the Buddha. The most striking example is the episode of the wounded swan. The biographical accounts tell us that the prince and his cousin Devadatta were wandering in the park that surrounded the royal residence when Devadatta shot down a swan with his bow and arrow. Both youths ran toward where the swan had fallen, but Siddhartha, being the faster runner, reached the place first. The young prince gathered the wounded bird up in his arms and sought to allay its suffering. Devadatta reacted angrily to this, insisting that the swan belonged to him, inasmuch as he had shot it down. The youths took their dispute to the wise man of the court, who decided to award the bird to Siddhartha on the grounds that life rightly belongs to him who would preserve it and not to him who would destroy it.

In this simple story, we have an excellent example of the Buddha's early manifestation of the attitude of love and compassion, an attitude whose object is to foster as far as possible the happiness of others and to allay their suffering. Later, also, after his enlightenment, the Buddha continued to demonstrate this attitude in remarkable ways. There is, for instance, the well-known episode wherein the Buddha took it upon himself to nurse the ailing monk Tissa. The latter's illness was such as caused all the other members of the Order to shun him. However, the Buddha, resolved to lead by example, personally cleaned and cared for Tissa's diseased and decaying body, thereby alleviating his suffering.

Last, let us take a long look at the attitude of wisdom, which is the most important of the three, being commensurate with enlightenment itself. It is wisdom that finally opens the door to freedom, and wisdom that removes ignorance, the fundamental cause of suffering. It is said that while one may sever the branches of a tree and even cut down its trunk, if the root is not removed, the tree will grow again. In a similar way, although one may remove attachment by means of renunciation, and aversion by means of love and compassion, as long as ignorance is not removed by means of wisdom, attachment and aversion are liable to arise again.

The principal instrument through which wisdom may be gained is meditation. Again, there is an event early in the Buddha's life in which his precocious skill in concentrating the mind is evident. According to the accounts of the life of Shakyamuni, immediately after witnessing the unhappy incident involving the worm and the bird at the plowing ceremony, the prince sat under a nearby rose-apple tree, and there spontaneously began to meditate, achieving the first level of meditation by concentrating his mind on the process of inhalation and exhalation. In this event we have evidence of a very early experience of meditation in the life of the Buddha.

Later, when he renounced the life of a householder and went forth to seek the ultimate truth, one of the first disciplines he developed was that of meditation. The accounts tell us that the ascetic Gotama (as he was known during his six years of striving for enlightenment) studied under two renowned teachers of meditation, Alara Kalama and Uddaka Ramaputta. Under the tutelage of these teachers he studied and mastered the various techniques of concentrating the mind.

And yet, remarkably, the ascetic Gotama left the two teachers in question because he found that meditation alone could not permanently put an end to suffering, even though it might supply temporary relief. This fact is important, because although the teaching of the Buddha emphasizes the practice of mental development and is therefore clearly in the tradition of the Indus Valley civilization, the Buddha transcended the limited goals of mere meditation and brought a new dimension to religious experience. This is what distinguishes the Buddha's teaching from the teaching of many other Indian schools, particularly those which, in one form or another, embrace the practice of yoga, or meditation.

In short, what distinguishes Buddhism from the contemplative traditions of Hinduism and other religions is the fact that, for Buddhism, meditation by itself is not enough. We might say that, for Buddhism, meditation is like sharpening a pencil. We sharpen a pencil for a purpose, let us say, in order to write. Similarly, by means of meditation we sharpen the mind for a definite purpose—in this case, the purpose is wisdom. The relationship between meditation and wisdom has also been explained with the help of the example of a torch. Suppose we want to see a picture on the wall of a darkened room with the aid of a torch. If the light cast by the torch is too dim, if the flame is disturbed by drafts of air, or if the hand holding the torch is unsteady, it is impossible to see the picture clearly. Similarly, if we want to penetrate the darkness of ignorance and see into the real nature of existence, we will be unable to do so if our minds are weak, distracted, and unsteady as a consequence of habitual indolence and emotional and intellectual disturbances. The Buddha put this discovery into practice on the night of his enlightenment. Then, we are told, he made his mind concentrated, one-pointed, and supple by means of meditation, directed it to the understanding of the real nature of things, and comprehended the truth. Therefore, the enlightenment of the Buddha was the consequence of the combination of meditation and wisdom.

There are also other dimensions of wisdom exemplified in the life of the Buddha. One of these is the understanding of the Middle Way. The conception of the Middle Way is central in Buddhism and has many levels of meaning, all of which it is not possible to consider here. However, this much may be said at once: The most fundamental meaning of the Middle Way is the avoidance of the extremes of indulgence in pleasures of the senses and, alternatively, tormenting the body. This fundamental aspect of the Middle Way is illustrated in the life of the Buddha by his very own career and experience. Before his renunciation of the life of a householder, Siddhartha enjoyed a life of luxury and sensual pleasure. Later, when he had become an ascetic in search of the truth, he spent six years practicing all manner of physical deprivations and self-mortification. Eventually, he understood the futility of such practices as well as the meaninglessness of his former life of indulgence, and discovered the Middle Way that avoids both extremes.

There are, of course, many other important episodes in the life of the Buddha that would be interesting and valuable to discuss, but my point in choosing to concentrate on these few elements is simply that we can begin to look at the Buddha's life as a lesson in conduct and concept, and not simply as a biography containing a number of names and places. Then we can appreciate the attitudes exemplified in Shakyamuni's career. In this way, a greater and more genuine insight into the real significance of the life of the Buddha becomes possible.

THE BUDDHA NATURE

By Khenpo Appey Rinpoche

It is said that in order to practice the Mahayana one must belong to the race of the Mahayana. According to the teaching also, all of us naturally have a race. The point is whether this race has been awakened in our mind. For some, this race has been awakened while for others it has not.

There are four signs to show that this race has been awakened:

When one has faith in the Triple Gem—the Buddha, the dharma and the sangha.
When one has compassion for other sentient beings.
When one has abandoned harming others and has patience no matter what arises.
When one has great desire to do virtuous deeds and accomplish virtue.

We can define the word race to mean Buddha nature or the cause of Buddhahood. It means that all sentient beings from beginningless time have the seed of enlightenment. However, there are unfavorable conditions or obstructions to the awakening of this "race" within us.

There are four categories of obstructions:

When we are completely under the power of the defilements so that whatever we do, we are under the power of hatred and desire. There is no thought of practicing the dharma.

When we are under the influence of bad friends and teachers. These people will give bad advice and will be an evil influence. Under such circumstances we will not be able to turn our mind to the dharma. A bad teacher who teaches the wrong path leads us away from the true teaching and obstructs us from going to other teachers who teach the true dharma.

Being in poverty—without food, clothing, shelter and other basic necessities. This completely obstructs us from entering the dharma.

When we are under the power of others we do not have any independence to think freely for ourselves. A great Indian scholar said that when a person was young he was under the power of his parents. He was not allowed to think for himself. When he grew to become a young man, he came under the power of his spouse. Later, when he became old, he came under the power of his children or grandchildren. He was never truly free to do what he wished to do. In all these cases, no matter who we are, we do not have freedom, and this obstructs the awakening of the Buddha nature within us.

Different Buddhist traditions discuss the idea of race in different ways. For example, the Cittamatra (Mind-Only) school teaches that there are three or four types of race. We can either enter into the race of the Arhats, the race of Pratiyeka Buddhas or the race of Buddhas and Bodhisattvas. In addition, some have even said that there is a race that is devoid of race, that some living things have no race and that they can never enter into any of these three paths to gain any form of enlightenment. However, the Madhyamika (Middle Way) school does not accept this idea of people without a race. They say that everyone has a race. Temporarily, one has the race of Arhats, Pratiyeka Buddhas or Bodhisattvas, but ultimately everyone will enter the final path of Buddhahood. Nonetheless, the Madhyamika accepts the idea that this world of existence is endless, is inexhaustible. Indirectly, it is tantamount to saying that some people will never get out of this world of existence.

There are two stories to illustrate this point on the difficulty of awakening the race within us. The first story is about Angulimala whose name means "the one who wears the garland of fingers." This happened during the time when the Buddha Shakyamuni was in the kingdom of Sarvasti whose king was Kusananji. In that place there was a great scholar who had many disciples. One day the king summoned the scholar to the palace. In order to keep watch over his house and also over his wife, the scholar left behind one of his disciples. This disciple had a name which means "one who is very pleasing to look at" because of the beauty of his body. The scholar's wife had great desire for the disciple, and when the scholar and his disciples were away she approached him in a very alluring way. However the boy told her that she was like a mother to him and he would not have anything to do with her. So in order to avoid her, the boy ran away.

The woman became very distressed after what the boy had done to her. She tore her clothes, scratched her body in many places, and beat herself with a stick. When her husband returned home she complained that his disciple had done all that to her when he was away. The scholar believed her and decided to destroy the boy. But he thought that as he was a very clever boy, he would need a very special method to destroy him. So he decided that he would tell the boy that it was through his actions that he had lost his caste of brahmin and also that he would never be able to gain liberation or gain a state of rebirth in heaven unless he rectified it by killing 1,000 people. He called the boy back and told him about that. At first the boy refused to do it as he felt that this could not be right. But the teacher convinced him that he must believe the teacher who was teaching him the ways of gaining proper understanding of things in this world.

Believing what his teacher had said, the boy Angulimala went out and killed 1,000 people. He went back to tell his teacher what he had done. But the scholar told him that he had to show proof of what he had done by cutting off the finger of those whom he had killed and to string them into a garland and wear it around his neck. The boy again went out and killed another 999 people.

At that time when he had already killed 999 people, his mother, being worried about his absence for many days went searching for him. When the boy saw his mother coming toward him, he thought that it was the time he would kill his mother and make her his 1,000th victim. He thought that he would then be able to gain the state of rebirth in heaven and would also be able to put his mother in heaven by killing her. So he drew out his knife and approached his mother.

The Buddha Shakyamuni, who was in that vicinity, had perceived what was happening through his omniscience. He saw that it was the right moment to place this boy on the dharma path and also to awaken his enlightenment thought. So the Buddha approached the boy and began to walk in front of him. The boy Angulimala found the Buddha's appearance very wonderful and called to him to stop. He asked the Buddha who he was who had the audacity to wander in front of him. The Buddha replied that he was the fully awakened one. He continued walking in front of Angulimala who asked him to stop as he had intention to kill the Buddha. The Buddha said to him that he was standing still and was not moving anywhere. He was always in the place where no one would ever harm anyone else. That was the place where he stayed, and that Angulimala must go and stay in such a place. That was the place where he would have the patience never to harm another living being. The Buddha told him that by then he should have realized that he had been tricked into following the wrong path which would lead to great suffering, that he was even about to kill his own mother who had, out of great kindness and compassion, come to help him.

Speaking in this way he was able to tame the mind of the boy and convinced him that he was in the wrong path. Angulimala took refuge in the Buddha and requested to become a monk to which the Buddha acceded. Through the Buddha's teaching which awakened his seed of virtue, Angulimala became an Arhat at that moment. He rose up to the sky and flew to the city of Sarvasti.

In the city of Sarvasti, the king was preparing his army to kill Angulimala because of what he had done. When the soldiers saw Angulimala coming down from the sky, they were scared and ran away. They reported to the king that Angulimala had come. The king at that moment thought he should ask the Buddha for advice regarding

Angulimala. The Buddha told him that Angulimala had gained the enlightenment of an Arhat and that the king need not be afraid of him anymore. The king thought that if the Buddha had such great power to help Angulimala to gain the state of Arhatship, he wondered why the Buddha did not do that before Angulimala had killed 1,999 people.

The Buddha explained by asking the king about the 500 people who worked for him as bird hunters. He asked the king why he did not stop them from killing when he had the power to stop them. The king thought that was quite right and told all his 500 hunters to stop killing birds from then on, and the punishment for breaking his order was death.

The 500 hunters got together and thought that the order did not apply to their sons. So they ordered their sons to go out to kill the birds since they did not fall under the ruling of the king. As they belonged to the race of slaughterers, they were not able to give up the idea of non-virtue. They would force their children to do it when they were not able to do so. This story refers to the idea that they were so steep in their non-virtues that no matter what was being done for them, nobody was able to stop their non-virtuous actions and awaken their race. However, it is said that at that time the Buddha performed a miraculous manifestation in front of them and gave them a teaching, and due to that they were able to correct their thinking and stopped themselves and their sons from further killing. So we can see that through the kindness of the Buddha, it is possible to awaken the race. This illustrates the point that there are many people who do not have the power at this time to awaken the race of enlightenment within themselves.

The second story is about a young Chinese boy whose family decided to send him to a temple one day. They told him that he was going to a temple which had many different images of the Buddha, Avalokiteshvara and others, and he should look at them carefully and learn to identify them. However, the boy did not like to do that. In fact, he had a great dislike for any image of the Buddhas or Bodhisattvas. So before entering the temple, he blindfolded his eyes to make sure that he would never see any of the images when he walked inside. No matter how much his parents forced him, he just refused to look.

Later, they thought of a way to overcome this. They put an image of the Bodhisattva Avalokiteshvara inside a vessel, covered it and put it in front of the boy. They told him that he must open the vessel and see the image of Avalokiteshvara. He should take it out and look at it. The boy was very angry to hear such a thing. He took a piece of cloth and tied it round his eyes and ears so that he could not see and hear. Having his hand wrapped around with another cloth, he picked up the vessel and threw it away. He had such a great dislike for the Buddha and his teachings that he would do anything possible to stay away, even to the extent of avoiding seeing the image. This illustrates the point of the difficulty of awakening the race within oneself.

THE FIVE PATHS TO ENLIGHTENMENT

By Khenpo Appey Rinpoche

It is not absolutely necessary to teach the five paths of the enlightened beings as well as the ten stages of enlightenment because we do not have that level of realization to understand the teaching. However, in order to explain properly the path to enlightenment, we should know about it. Just as for example when we wish to travel to some other countries we would want to know about the place like its climate, customs, etc. so that we can prepare or adjust ourselves properly. In the same way, the five paths and the ten stages of enlightenment are taught in order to accustom ourselves with the path that we undertake. It is for this reason that it is necessary to teach these aspects of the enlightenment path.

The five paths refer to the path that one must traverse in order to gain the result of enlightenment.

The Path of Accumulation—The first path that one must travel is the path of accumulation. The path of accumulation refers to the idea when one begins to meditate on selflessness. In other words, the path of accumulation and the meditation on selflessness are here merged together.

The five paths are taught differently in the Hinayana and the Mahayana teachings.

According to the Mahayana teaching, in regard to the first path of accumulation, there are three paths—the smaller path of accumulation, the middle path of accumulation, and the great path of accumulation. The small path of accumulation means that through meditating or progressing on this path there is no certainty as to the time when we will arrive at the second of the five paths that is the path of application. The middle path of accumulation means that there is a definite idea of time when we will reach the path of application. And the great path of accumulation means that in this very lifetime, with this very body that we have, we will gain the second path of application.

When it is asked who is able to gain this first path, the path of accumulation, according to the Hinayana teachings, they say only a human being of this world who is either a male or a female is able to gain this path of accumulation. No other living being in this world such as a god, an animal, or a human being who does not have the proper organs is able to gain this stage of accumulation. According to the Mahayana, it is said that there are other sentient beings besides human beings in this world who are able to gain this first path of accumulation.

It is also asked whether it is necessary to have a mind which can be placed in concentration meditation in order to gain this first path of accumulation. It is said that it is not necessary because even those within the realm of desire who do not have this mind of concentration meditation have been able to accomplish this first path of accumulation. Again, it is asked whether it is necessary to have a mind which can go into different states of Dhyanas or meditative trances. It is said that there are some whose minds have not been placed in any of the Dhyanas who have gained the path of accumulation. So it is not necessary that the mind must be first placed in one of these states of meditation in order to accomplish the path of accumulation.

It is said that when a person through the motivation of compassion takes the vows of the enlightenment thought and begins to practice in accordance with that enlightenment thought, he has entered into the path of accumulation at that time. When we enter into the path of accumulation there are many practices which we must perform. There are five special qualities which the person who is practicing the first path of accumulation should have. Actually there are many different qualities but we can combine them into five principal qualities:

The first quality is to have proper moral conduct. This means that you hold the vows that you have taken either as a monk, nun or lay person.

The second quality is to maintain the proper use of our senses through wisdom and method. This means that whatever we are relating with through our senses, such as forms through our eyes, or sound through our ears, through the door of wisdom we see that they are really of the nature of emptiness. In regard to method, here it means that whatever we do in this life we are always purifying all our actions into a quality of enlightenment. For example, when we walk down the street, at that time we purify this by the thought, "As I walk down this street, may all sentient beings enter into the path of enlightenment," or when you close the door before you "May all sentient beings close the door to the lower realms." So in this way, we purify the objects that we encounter with our senses.

The third quality is not to have great attachment to our food. Here it means that someone who is practicing this path of accumulation does not become attached to the food or eat food with the thought of desire. In other words, we have a proper perception as to why we are eating food. We should have the thought that we eat in order to benefit or to feed the different types of worms in our body, or that we are eating in order to sustain this body that we have, so as to make it a proper vessel for the practice of dharma. Through various methods such as these, we have a proper idea of why we are eating and we do not create great attachment to the food we have and also we eat in moderation.

The fourth quality is that we do not sleep excessively. Instead we should devote part of our waking hours like the early part of the night and the early part of the morning for the purpose of meditation. With a very stable and steady mind we could meditate for example on the impurities of the human body, on the four states of mindfulness of body, sensation, mind, dharma, and also on the various aspects of the enlightenment thought.

The fifth quality is to have conscientiousness or awareness of what should be done and what should not be done. It means that someone of this path has not only mindfulness but also awareness. When he is involved in a certain deed or actions, he should at that time know which is a proper deed and which is an improper deed, which one has faults and which one has benefits. He should know it at the time the deed is being done, not before or after, and then acts in accordance with the proper understanding.

These are just some of the qualities of the person who is practicing the path of accumulation. It is said that when someone reaches the stage of the great path of accumulation, one is able to gain certain forms of miraculous power or supernatural power by which one can even go to different Buddha realms in order to receive the teachings or listen to the teachings of various Buddhas and Bodhisattvas.

The main practice within the path of accumulation is listening or studying the dharma and also contemplation. There are some practices within the first path of accumulation in regard to meditation. However, the principal practices here primarily deal with study and contemplation. The Sanskrit word for accumulation is Sambhara. This means that one must practice virtue again and again in order to accomplish the virtue or the merit by which one will really gain the path. Accumulation means accumulating merit or accumulating virtue, the continuous and constant practice of virtue. This is the main practice within the first path of accumulation.

The Path of Application—The second path is the path of application. The path of application refers to the mind which meditates on emptiness or selflessness. On this stage we do not yet have the actual realization of emptiness or selflessness. However, we have a thought about selflessness, or we have a concept of selflessness. Actually, when we consider this thought or this idea about selflessness, we work with that, we meditate on that. This itself is known as the path of application. Just as for example, although we have not gone to a certain place but as we know about the place, we meditate on the things we know about that place, in the same way, at this time, though we do not have a realization of emptiness or selflessness, we work on the meaning behind it. This is what we work with at this path of application.

The three paths of application—the small path of

application, the middle path of application, and the great path of application are similar to those of the path of accumulation. When there is no definite time as to when we will gain the next path which is the path of seeing, that is known as the small path of application. The middle path means that there is a certain time or definite time when we will gain the third path of seeing, and the great path of application means that in this very lifetime, with this very body we will gain the third path of seeing.

The path of application can also be divided into four parts, into what is known as heat, foremost, patience and the highest dharma.

Based on the accumulation of merit achieved on the path of accumulation, we begin to meditate on emptiness. Before we have the realization of emptiness, it is sort of like before we have a fire, heat starts to appear, and as the heat increases, then the fire bursts out. So in the same way, in our meditation on emptiness, before we really have the realization of emptiness, it is like a pile of heat which arises before that state. It is like a lesser form of meditation on emptiness. So when we are able to start to produce this heat which will later blaze into the correct meditation on emptiness, this is known as the first stage of the path of application.

When our meditation on emptiness increases, though we still do not have the realization at that time, but the heat arising from that is increasing, or in other words, our mind is being steadied in that type of meditation, this is known as the foremost.

Then when we are able to increase our level of meditation and have no fear of the meditation on emptiness, we have the patience toward the meditation itself. It has become a bearable meditation and not something that we are afraid of anymore. This is known as patience.

When we are able to overcome any form of fear through this meditation on emptiness, in other words, we overcome different types of conceptualization arising to obstruct us from gaining this realization of emptiness, then we get to the fourth stage, which is known as the highest dharma or the most excellent dharma. However, our realization of emptiness is still not accomplished at this stage. We have accomplished all the various types of worldly dharmas but the transcendental dharma of the state of realization of emptiness has not been obtained. So at this point, everything up to this stage has been accomplished.

Again, when it is asked who can obtain the stage of the path of application, according to the Hinayana or ordinary teaching, it is said that anyone within this world of existence born as a man or woman with proper organs and also anyone within the first six heavenly states of the realm of desire is able to gain this path of application. According to the Madhyamika teaching or the Mahayana teaching, it is said that besides these, there are others also who are able to gain this path of application.

When it is asked who is able to meditate on the state of the path of application, it is said that only those who have gained one of the four states of Dhyana which again is sub-divided into six types of meditation found in the realm of form. Anyone who has attained one of these states of meditation is able to accomplish or dwell within this path of application.

In regard to what is realized within this path of application, according to the Hinayana teaching, it is the nature of the Four Noble Truths which is also divided into sixteen aspects with each of the Four Noble Truths having four aspects such as the aspect of selflessness, etc. The sixteen aspects of the Four Noble Truths are realized at this time.

According to certain of the Mahayana teachings, such as the Mind-Only school, it is said that during the first two parts of this path of application, during the time of heat and the time of the foremost, there is a realization of non-grasping at the objects of this world or of objective reality. And at the time of patience and the foremost dharma, there is a state of the non-grasping of the subjective reality.

According to some teachers such as Nagarjuna, they said that when a person meditates at the time of the path of application, there is no separate arising of realization such as non-grasping of object and non-grasping of subject. Though the realization of emptiness is not complete, the wisdom arising from the meditation on emptiness increases through these four aspects of heat, foremost, patience, and highest dharma. This actually produces greater stability on the understanding of the meditation of emptiness, though it is not completely realized at that point.

Also, according to the Hinayana teachings, they say that the third of these four paths of application, which is the path of patience, has three aspects—the small, the middle and the great, but the other three paths only has one single aspect. However, according to the Mahayana, they say that each of these four paths have the three aspects of small, middle and great, that in total there are twelve different levels or stages within this path of application.

The Sanskrit word for application is parayogamarga. "Para" means ultimate truth or ultimate reality. "Yoga" means to join or to unite. So parayogamarga means the path which unites with ultimate reality. In other words, this second path which we have translated as the path of application or the path of uniting means the meditation which will unite us with the realization of the stage of ultimate reality which arises at the third path, the path of seeing. In other words, through the path of application all the requisites and also the joining together for the realization which will arise at the next stage, the path of seeing is being accomplished.

The Path of Seeing—The path of seeing means to see the nature of the Four Noble Truths, to realize the nature of ultimate reality, to awaken within one's own mind the transcendental wisdom which directly perceives the nature of all phenomena. The path of seeing can also be classified into three types—the path of seeing of the Hinayana, the Pratiyeka Buddhayana, and the Mahayana. In order to accomplish the path of seeing, we must relinquish the approximate cause and then the cause itself. The approximate cause means, for example, if desire is created this is what needs to be abandoned. And then we need to destroy the cause of desire. Generally, this is classified as what needs to be abandoned in relation to seeing and what needs to be abandoned in relation to meditation.

In relation to what needs to be abandoned on the path of seeing, what needs to be abandoned are the ten defilements—the six basic defilements such as desire, hatred, pride, doubt, and ignorance and then the five secondary defilements which constitute the sixth basic defilement of wrong view. Also, in relation to each of these ten, there are the three realms of existence—the realm of desire, form realm and formless realm, and the Four Noble Truths. In total, there are 112 different aspects to be abandoned. This is according to the Abhidharmasamucaya or the Abhidharma teaching of the Mahayana. According to the Abhidharmakosa of the Hinayana, there are said to be 88 aspects that need to be abandoned.

According to the Mahayana teachings, at the time of meditation there arises on the stage of the first Bhumi the path of seeing. In other words, the path of seeing is equated with the first Bhumi. What needs to be abandoned can be categorized into two parts–the obscuration of the afflictions or defilements, and also the obscuration of knowable things. These two major obscurations need to be destroyed in order to gain firstly, liberation and then full and perfect enlightenment.

It is said that at the time of meditation on the path of seeing, the realization that arises destroys at that very moment all the obscuration of the defilements completely. And in regard to the obscuration of knowable things which can be divided into two sections—what should be abandoned in relation to seeing, and what should be abandoned in relation to meditation, the first of these is also destroyed at the time of meditation on the path of seeing.

Regarding who can gain this stage of seeing, according to the Hinayana teaching, it is said that any male or female within this world of existence as well as any gods within the first six lower heavenly realms are able to gain this path of seeing. According to the Mahayana, not only that, but even animals and others are able to gain this path of seeing.

In order to gain this stage of the path of seeing, first of all, we must be able to gain some form of samadhi, and then based on that samadhi one is able to gain realization into the path of seeing. According to the Hinayana, they say that in relation to the four Dhyanas, the first Dhyana has three parts and the remaining three has one part each. So there are six forms of meditation or Dhyana that one can gain. One needs only to have gained samadhi of any one of the six before one can gain realization into the path of seeing. However, according to the Pratiyeka Buddha teaching and also the Mahayana, it is said that one must gain meditation of the fourth Dhyana, the highest form of Dhyana before one is able to gain realization into the path of seeing.

In regard to what is realized on the path of seeing, according to the Hinayana what they realize is seeing the Four Noble Truths as the objects of meditation and based on those Four Noble Truths they proceed to realize the stage of selflessness in relation to the person. So the personal "I" is seen to be selfless. There is no self in relation to the person. For the Pratiyeka Buddha, in addition to the realization of the selflessness of the person, he realizes also the objective aspect of the selflessness of all phenomena. For the Bodhisattva, at the path of seeing, not only does he have realization of the selflessness of the person and the realization of the objective aspect of the selflessness of all phenomena, but also the subjective aspect of the selflessness of all phenomena which is the mind which perceives all phenomena. In other words, a complete realization of emptiness.

According to the Hinayana teaching, all phenomena are seen to be empty individually. According to the Mahayana, all phenomena, both the personal self and external phenomena, everything in one moment is seen to be completely void of any true nature. In other words, the empty nature which completely transcends all conceptualization or all mental creation is completely realized on the path of seeing.

The path of seeing is known as Darshanamarga in Sanskrit. It means to see something for the first time, to see in proper light the truth of the Four Noble Truths and the emptiness of all phenomena. Through obtaining the path of seeing, according to the Mahayana one gains the first Bhumi, one becomes a first stage Bodhisattva or Noble One. The Hinayana tradition does not have this idea of the ten Bhumis. However, the realization that arises at the path of seeing turns one into an Arya or a noble person. According to them, there are different forms of noble persons, different types of realizations that they gain, and this is different from the Mahayana.

The Path of Meditation—The fourth path is the path of meditation. Here meditation means that having seen ultimate reality, the realization obtained at the path of seeing, this must be meditated upon again and again in order to make it stable, to make it a habitual pattern in one's own mind so that it really becomes a part of one's being. For the path of meditation, there are two types of meditation—the worldly meditation and the transcendental or the unworldly meditation. In relation to the worldly meditation, there are meditations on the four states of meditation or Dhyanas in relation to the realm of form and also the four Dhyanas in relation to the formless realm. For each of these states there are seven preparatory steps. When the seven preparatory steps of each state are accomplished, then the respective state of mediation or Dhyana is accomplished.

In order to make the mind very firm, to establish a proper state of meditation within the mind, these worldly meditations, whichever one of them, if not all, must be accomplished in order to accomplish the path. This teaching on the different states of meditation in relation to the form and formless realms is very important and there are many commentaries written on it.

The transcendental type of meditation means to accustom or habituate the mind to the realization at the time of the path of seeing. At the time of the path of seeing, when the realization of emptiness arises, it only arises at the time of meditation itself. The meditator can see it only at the time of meditation. However, all these meditative states have two aspects, at the time of sitting in meditation, and at the time after one comes out of the meditation, during one's daily life when many different things will arise in the mind. At the time of the path of seeing, the realization of emptiness only arises at the time of meditation and not after the meditation.

The transcendental path of meditation seeks to habituate the mind with the realization of emptiness so that it not only adheres within one's mind during the meditation but also during one's daily life. This is what is meditated on and this again can be seen in relation to the three types of yana—the Hinayana, Pratiyeka Buddhayana and the Mahayana. According to the common path teaching, there are 14 different aspects that must be abandoned at this time in order to accomplish the path of meditation.

In regard to who can accomplish the path of meditation, it is said that someone who is born in this world of existence either as a male or female, also, anyone who is

born within the six lower realms of desire. And within the
form and formless realm, someone who has not fallen into the
state of Brahma, but who has gained a meditative state known
as the state of perception which arises at the fourth Dhyana.

In regard to the state of meditation that we must
have in order to gain the path of meditation, according to
the Hinayana, the type of meditation that is required is the
six Dhyanas or samadhi. The first Dhyana which is divided
into three Dhyanas together with the second, third and
fourth Dhyana and also the first three stages of the
meditative state of the formless realm. Someone who has
gained samadhi of all these can gain meditation into the
transcendental path of meditation. According to the
Pratiyeka Buddhayana and the Mahayana, just by gaining
the four Dhyanas is sufficient.

The Sanskrit word for the path of meditation is
Bhavanamarga. This means habituating or accustoming the
mind again and again. According to the Mahayana teaching
each of the ten Bhumis has two aspects—the realization
which arises during the meditation and the subsequent
realization which arises after the meditation. The third path
of seeing means that on the first stage of enlightenment, the
first Bhumi, only the first aspect is accomplished. In other
words, only during meditation does one see the emptiness
of all things. However, the subsequent attainment arising
out of that meditation does not occur until one has gained
the next path which is the path of meditation. And the path
of meditation itself includes the second part of the first
Bhumi up to and including the entire 10 Bhumis. So it
means that the meditative states and the subsequent
attainments within the ten Bhumis are accomplished within
this fourth path of meditation.

The Path of No More Learning—The fifth path is called the path of complete accomplishment or the path of no more learning, that we do not have to learn anything anymore. This means that the result and path are merged together. In other words, the result of what we are seeking to gain is gained here. So for example, if one is practicing the Hinayana path, it means that at this stage one gains what the Hinayana defines as the complete path of accomplishment, that one becomes an Arhat. If one is practicing the Pratiyeka Buddha teaching, one who has accomplished this fifth stage is known as a Pratiyeka Buddha. According to the Mahayana, this fifth stage is known as the stage of Buddhahood.

When it is asked who is able to gain this stage and what type of meditation is required, according to the common teaching, anyone who is born in this world whether male or female, also, anyone living in the six lower heavenly realms of the realm of desire, or the form or formless realm, but has not been born as god Brahma. According to the Pratiyeka Buddha teaching, one must be a human being. According to the Mahayana, in order to gain the stage of Buddhahood, not only must one be a human being, one must be born in Jambudvipa, the southern continent of this world of existence. In addition, one must belong to one of the two higher classes of Brahmin or Chetriya.

Also, in regard to the meditation that is needed, according to the Hinayana teaching, anyone with the six Dhyanas and also any of the first three meditative states of the formless realm. According to the Pratiyeka Buddha tradition and the Mahayana, the kind of meditation that is needed is that one must have gained the fourth Dhyana.

It is said that at the time of the path of application, when one arises from the meditation on the excellent dharma, one actually flows into the realization of the path of seeing. In other words, one sees the true nature of all dharmas. In the same way, on the stage of the tenth Bhumi, one practices at that time the seeing meditation of the tenth Bhumi as well as accomplishes the attainments that come after that, that the various qualities in relation to these two are meditated upon again and again until the qualities are completely accomplished. When they are completely accomplished, in a natural flow, if one enters into the next stage of meditation which is known as the samadhi that is like a diamond or vajra, and then arising from that stage one actually gains the result of complete Buddhahood.

The fifth path of no more learning is known in Sanskrit as Nisthamarga which means that all the qualities of enlightenment are completely gained. There is then no need to study or meditate or accomplish anything as everything is now completely accomplished.

THE TEN BHUMIS TO ENLIGHTENMENT

By Khenpo Appey Rinpoche

The word "stage" or "Bhumi" means the level of attainments. This teaching on the Bhumi is presented differently in the Hinayana and the Mahayana. Within the Hinayana teaching, there are eight levels or stages of Bhumi that can be attained. Within the Mahayana, the stages of the Bhumi are divided into two parts—the stage of ordinary worldly people and the stage of the enlightened ones. And the stage of the enlightened ones means the ten stages of the Bodhisattva path.

It is sometimes asked why there are only ten stages of the Bodhisattva path and not less or more. The reason for this is that though the realization of ultimate reality arising from each of the ten stages is the same, the quality that arises from the subsequent practices are many. Here, in order to gain the qualities of the subsequent practices of the Bodhisattva path, the practitioner must accomplish the ten perfections. And these ten perfections relate to the ten stages of the Bodhisattva path. Also, because the Bodhisattva must take different births and engage in different practices, so it is said that there are ten different qualities to be gained and ten different kinds of abandonments to be relinquished.

In relation to each of these ten stages, each one has something that must be abandoned and also something that has to be gained. For example, by gaining the first stage of the Bodhisattva path, it is said that one is always free from all suffering like old age, sickness and disease. And especially, one is free from the five different types of fear:

Fear of worrying about where one is going to get one's food for one's livelihood.

Fear about death, that we are going to die.

Fear of being born in the lower realms.

Fear of worrying about people criticizing us or blaming us.

Fear of the different things that people are talking about.

In relation to the attainments that are obtained on the various stages, there are many different qualities that are obtained. However, we can classify them into twelve different attainments. On the stage of the first Bhumi, there are 100 of each of these. For example, we gain the attainment of having a special type of body and with that body we can emanate 100 different bodies at one moment. Also each of these 100 bodies will have 100 disciples listening to the teaching, and one is able to see 100 Buddhas at one time. One is able to perform miracles in 100 different realms or world spheres at the same time.

Then, with the second Bhumi the attainments are similar but the number is increased. So within the second Bhumi, this number is 1,000, and then with the third Bhumi, the number is 10,000. So there is the progression in number of how many people one can liberate or how many bodies one can emanate.

The word Bhumi literally means "earth" or "ground." Sometimes, it is translated as the ten earths or the ten stages or the ten grounds. The reason that this word is used to illustrate the stages of the Bodhisattva is that just like the earth or ground is able to support or to hold many things both animate and inanimate, in the same way, the ten Bhumis are able to maintain many different qualities which are obtained by the person who has gained these different stages of enlightenment.

From the dharma point of view, when we look at its essence, the word Bhumi means the stages of realization which is the combination of the understanding of the true nature of all phenomena with the thought of compassion for all sentient beings. In other words, when the wisdom of the realization of emptiness and compassion are merged, this is known as the stage of enlightenment.

The first Bhumi is known as "the very joyful stage." The reason this is called joyful is that those who have gained that realization at that time know definitely that they will be able to gain the stage of full and perfect enlightenment. They therefore know that they will gain very great benefit for themselves. Also, they know that they will be able to help many sentient beings through their realization. Due to this realization, their mind becomes very happy and very joyful.

The second Bhumi is called "the stainless" or freedom from impure moral conduct. The reason for this is that the emphasis at this time is on the perfection of moral conduct since it is through moral conduct that one is able to gain freedom from faults.

The third Bhumi refers to being able to teach the dharma to many people. This is similar to light rays going out to pervade the world. So the third stage is known as "the issuing of light rays."

The fourth Bhumi is like the idea of making light rays and this refers to the increase in one's realization of transcendental wisdom. Though it is the same as the third stage, at this stage it has increased to a more thorough realization of the ultimate wisdom. For this reason, it is called "making light rays."

The fifth Bhumi is known as "the purification of difficulties." Here it means that when we are working for sentient beings, generally it is very difficult because whenever we do good to others we often get something bad in return. When we try very hard to work for other sentient beings, we have to face many difficulties. However, to the Bodhisattva who has effortless purified activities, he does not find any difficulty working for sentient beings. That is why this fifth stage is known as the "purification of difficulties."

The sixth Bhumi is known as "direct manifestation." This refers to the stage of the perfection of wisdom, the real perfection of wisdom itself. One really comes face to face with wisdom at this time and there is direct perception so that the wisdom and one's mind are really merged together.

The seventh Bhumi is known as "going to a far distance." This means that having gone across all the grasping to duality or having gone across the discriminating mind that is always discriminating different things, thinking that this is a male, this is a female, this is white, this is blue, etc. At this stage, we have gone beyond all the discrimination and our mind does not grasp at the subject/object duality anymore. Since it has passed all that it means that it has gone a very far distance.

These first seven stages are known as the impure seven stages of the Bodhisattva. The reason for this is that there is still a form of grasping in the mind during these seven stages.

The eighth Bhumi is known as "the unshakeable" or "the unmovable." This means that the enlightened mind does not need to conceptualize or create mental thoughts anymore. So this idea of conceptualization has been overcome and the mind is placed in an unshakeable stage that does not fall into the extremes of conceptualization.

The ninth Bhumi is known as "good intelligence." Here it means that the mind has gained a very pure state of realization or a very pure state of intelligence. It is said that the four different qualities of transcendental intelligence arise at this point.

The tenth Bhumi is known as "the cloud of dharma." This means that just as a big cloud which is filled with water can rain over big areas, similarly, the one who has attained this stage has the ability of not forgetting anything about the dharma. His mind or his realization is like a huge cloud which does not forget anything, all the dharmas and also all the different types of samadhi that it holds together.

THE QUALITIES OF THE BUDDHA

By *Khenpo Appey Rinpoche*

What is meant by one who is known as a Buddha? Here it refers to someone who has abandoned all the faults or impurities and also who has gained all the realizations. The impurities refer to all the defilements such as desire, hatred and ignorance and also what we can call the two obscurations—obscuration to the defilements and obscuration of knowable things. Knowable things means mental conceptualization which binds us to this world of subject and object duality. So the enlightened one or the Buddha has completely overcome every defilement from every point of view as well as all impure thoughts or conceptualization.

When we have overcome the defilements, sometimes there is still residue remaining behind. But the Buddha has not only overcome the root or source of all these impurities but also their residues. So for that reason he is said to be the one who has the perfection of the complete relinquishment or abandonment of all impurities.

Complete realization refers to the quality of knowing the true nature of all phenomena as well as knowing all phenomena exactly as they are according to their form or manifestation. Actually, realization has two aspects—one is to know what things are according to its ultimate nature, and the other is to discriminate or know all things as they are. The Buddha has both of these qualities. He knows everything in

36

this world just as it is, as well as the true nature of everything. This type of wisdom is known as complete perfection of realization or complete perfection of wisdom.

What we have just described is known as the defining characteristics of the term Buddha. It means that he has the qualities of abandonment and the qualities of realization. In addition to the defining characteristics, there is discussion of the body of the Buddha and also the qualities of the Buddha.

The Body of the Buddha

The body of the Buddha can be discussed in different ways. It is said that there are three different bodies of enlightenment which the Buddha possesses and these can be combined into two different bodies.

The first body can either be known as the Dharmakaya or the Svabhavakaya. The Dharmakaya means the body of the truth, and the Svabhavakaya means the essence body or the body of essential nature. The Dharmakaya means that the Buddha has complete realization of the true nature of all phenomena which is empty by nature. So it means complete purity of all stains or impurities in the mind; the mind which gains a complete state of purity, pure of all defilements or conceptualization. The mind of emptiness or the true nature of emptiness is known as the essential nature of the mind.

However, that alone does not constitute the Dharmakaya. Not only is the realization of the nature of all phenomena to be empty, but also merged together with this is the mind of the Buddha which is known as the transcendental wisdom. This means that the ordinary mind that we have as ordinary people at the time of enlightenment is transformed from an impure mind into the pure mind of wisdom. So the Buddha's mind is not a clouded mind like ours but instead it is completely transformed into the transcendental wisdom or primordial wisdom. Actually, there are many names for it, like primordial awareness or wisdom, transcendental wisdom or knowledge. But this quality of transcendental wisdom and also the understanding of the empty nature of the mind are indistinguishable from each other. When they are merged together, this is known as the Dharmakaya or the body of truth.

The second body of enlightenment is known as the Sambhogakaya which means the body of enjoyment. This refers to an emanation body or physical body which resides in the pure Buddha realm of Akanishta. And within that realm this body appears with the various marks of perfection like the 32 major and 80 minor marks of enlightenment. Also, only the Mahayana teachings are taught by one who possesses that body. Also, only the Bodhisattvas on the tenth stage of enlightenment are able to see this body. This form is only manifested to help certain Bodhisattvas to progress along the path.

The third body which is known as the Nirmanakaya means the emanation body. Emanation means that many bodies can issue out or emanate from this essence of enlightenment of the Buddha. It means that just as the world of existence is as vast or limitless as space, so also sentient beings are as limitless and inconceivable as space. So in order to help all the sentient beings to gain the stage of liberation or enlightenment, an emanation body will manifest itself at any place, at any time and also in any form as long as sentient beings remain in this world of existence.

This emanating form which can take any shape or be born in any place or at any time is known as the Nirmanakaya.

Also, it is said that there are three different types of Nirmanakaya:

The first type is known as "birth Nirmanakaya" which is like the emanation body which resides in the Tushita heaven waiting to take birth in this world for the last time. It is like the case of the Buddha Shakyamuni before he took birth in this world.

The second type is known as "excellent Nirmanakaya" and this refers to one like our Buddha Shakyamuni who takes form in this world and displays the attainment of enlightenment and works for sentient beings, teaching the dharma.

The third type is known as "manufactured Nirmanakaya." This means any form which is necessary to help sentient beings such as the shape of a dancer or the shape of any other form besides the form of a Buddha.

If it is asked whether the Buddha has a mind, the answer is that the Buddha does not have mind like the mind we have that arises due to delusion. The Buddha has no delusion. He has completely overcome all delusion and being free from delusion, he cannot have a mind like ours which is just something that is functioning due to being under the state of delusion. Since the Buddha is not under any state of delusion, he is said to be free from the mind of delusion. So in that sense the Buddha does not have a mind.

If it is asked whether the Buddha has transcendental wisdom or awareness, the answer is that he has transcendental wisdom because anything that is put to the Buddha, anything that we request from the Buddha, he is able to give an answer due to his omniscience. The transcendental wisdom is the ordinary mind that has been transformed at the time of enlightenment. It is therefore not an ordinary mind anymore as it is completely changed into a quality of enlightenment, a state of realization which is free from all faults. Since the Buddha possesses this quality, one can say that the Buddha possesses transcendental wisdom and not the mind.

The three bodies of the Buddha can be condensed into what is known as the two bodies of enlightenment. The two bodies are the Dharmakaya and the Rupakaya. The Rupakaya are the two physical forms—the Sambhogakaya and the Nirmanakaya. "Rupa" means form, and "kaya" means body, so Rupakaya means the form body. However the meaning of these is the same. It is only different ways of classifying them.

Qualities of the Buddha

With regard to the third idea of the qualities of the Buddha, there are many verses written concerning this in the Mahayanasutralankara. Beside this, there are two special prayers or praises to the Buddha which describe his many special qualities. One was written by Maitreya and the other by Sakya Pandita. It is said that if one were to recite these texts daily one is able to gain a very great merit.

First of all, when we talk about the qualities of the Buddha we can say that the Buddha has limitless qualities. Here we can define the idea of limitless qualities in relation to two different intentions of the Buddha. One is to bring temporary benefit to sentient beings which is known as an intention of happiness, and the other is to bring ultimate benefit to sentient beings and this is known as the intention of benefit.

For example, when we look at the four Limitless Meditations, the first phrase "May all sentient being have happiness and the causes of happiness" relates to loving-kindness. The second phrase "May all sentient beings be free from suffering and the causes of suffering" relates to compassion. The third phrase "May all sentient beings have that state of happiness which is completely free from all suffering" relates to the state of joy. These three refer to the Buddha's intention of bringing temporary happiness to all sentient beings.

The fourth phrase "May all sentient beings live in equanimity, having neither attachment to loved ones nor hatred toward others," which is a balanced state of mind, refers to the Buddha's intention of bringing ultimate happiness to all. So in this way, in relation to the Limitless Meditations, the Buddha has what is known as these limitless qualities of benefiting all living beings both temporarily and ultimately.

The Buddha is also said to have the quality of the eight liberations or legends. It means different states of meditation or samadhi. Ordinary people in this world can gain some of these samadhi, such as the different qualities of overcoming some of the defilements. The Arhats and the Pratiyeka Buddhas can also gain these different qualities of samadhi by which they can overcome all the defilements. However, they do not overcome the obscuration of knowable things. The fully enlightened Buddha has fully all the eight qualities of samadhi because his mind has gained a state of meditation by which all the obscurations of defilements and knowable things are completely abandoned or overcome.

The Eighteen Special Qualities of the Buddha According to Maitreya

According to Maitreya, the first quality which the Buddha possesses is known as "dignified suppression." Just as the sun can in a dignified and majestic way suppress the stars in the sky, in that when the sun is shining we are not able to see the stars even though they are still there, in the same way, through different states of samadhi or meditation the Buddha can do various miracles in order to help all sentient beings. Though others may be able to do some of these, they are not able to do it in such a magnificent or wonderful manner that the Buddha is able to. And even when they do it, when the Buddha performs the miracles, the others are completely suppressed in that their quality becomes insignificant in relation to the Buddha's quality.

The second quality is known as "the ten exhaustions." This refers again to the different qualities of the Buddha's mind or the Buddha's transcendental wisdom and also his activities in the sense that the Buddha can, through certain meditative states, do different types of miracles. Also, he is able to know all the things in this world through his transcendental wisdom or omniscience. Though others are able to perform certain miracles or know to some extent different things in this world, no one is able to know everything in this world. The Buddha is able to know each and every individual phenomenon in this world and in its entirety. By the inexhaustible realization of the Buddha this vastness is known as exhausting the other states.

The third quality of the Buddha is known as "the destruction of the defilements." This means that for example, when someone produces in his mind desire, hatred or some other defilements, and he happens to see an Arhat, the Arhat is able, through his meditation, to stop him from having that one particular defilement. So if someone is angry with him he is able to stop the anger directed toward him. He can however only stop or suppress the one defilement that is directed at him. In the case of the Buddha, if someone sees him and was to create desire or hatred toward him, the Buddha is able to destroy all their defilements through his meditation.

The fourth quality of the Buddha is known as "arising or knowing from prayer." It means, for example when the Arhat is asked about the future, he does not need to predict or to throw dice. All he needs to do is to go into a state of samadhi and with effort he is able to give an answer about the future. However, if the Buddha is asked the same question, he does not need to engage in any effort to think about it like going into a state of samadhi. Without any hesitation or effort, he is able to give an answer. Moreover, the Arhats are able to know only some things about the future; the Buddha is able to know everything. For that reason, the Buddha is able to dispel all doubts.

The fifth quality of the Buddha is known as "the four pure intelligences or pure intellects:"

The first intelligence refers to knowing all things in this world according to each individual's capacity. For example, the Buddha knows what a pillar is or what a house is. He can identify each thing in this world individually.

He can identify the purpose of each thing. He knows its individual capacity or what its function or purpose is. For example, the efficacy of a pillar in holding up the beams. He knows each and every defining characteristic of every phenomenon in this world.

He is able to give a name to each and every thing.

He has no fear in telling people what the different things in the world are.

The sixth quality of the Buddha is known as "the supernatural consciousness or supernatural powers." There are six different supernatural powers that the Buddha has:

He is able to perform various miracles through his own meditative state.

He is able to know the mind of others, whether the person has defilement or not.

He has clairaudience. He can hear any sound from anywhere, even from the end of the universe. He has a supernatural power of hearing.

He is able to see and to know his own past lives as well as those of other living beings in this world.

He has clairvoyance. This specifically refers to the Buddha being able to see the future births of other living beings, where their births will take place.

He has the quality that is known as the exhaustion of defiled states. In order to help other living beings the Buddha knows the specific method by which they can overcome their defilements and gain a state of liberation.

The seventh quality which the Buddha possesses is known as "the major and minor marks of perfection." In English, we use the words "marks of perfection." In Tibetan, they are known as "the signs of perfection." It means that anyone who has the 32 major and 80 minor marks physically on his body means that that person has gained a state of holiness. An example of the major marks is the bump on the top of the head, and an example of the minor marks is the slight copperish color of the fingernails.

The purpose of having these is that whoever sees the person who has these marks of perfection will create faith in their mind and turn their mind with devotion to this person.

The eighth quality is known as "the four purities:"

The first purity is the purity of the basis or body. This means that taking birth in this world, staying in this world, and also passing away from this world, all these are done through free will. In other words, the Buddha has the choice of when to take birth and how long to stay in the world.

The second purity is the purity of object. This means that the Buddha has complete control over various objective realities in this world. For example, he can make things that are in existence to disappear, and things that are not in existence to appear, or do whatever he wants with them in order to help sentient beings.

The third purity is the purity of mind. This means the enlightened mind of the Buddha. It refers to the power of the Buddha's mind to enter into different samadhis and to use them at will. So he has complete power over the different meditative states.

The fourth purity is the purity of transcendental wisdom. This means that the Buddha has accomplished the complete realization of all transcendental knowledge. And by this he has the power over all transcendental wisdom.

The ninth quality of the Buddha is known as "the ten powers." These ten powers are specifically in relation to different types of power of realization or knowledge:

The first power is known as "the power of residing." This means that the Buddha knows how things should reside in this world, how they appear and how they cannot appear in this world. Just as water can only flow or abide on a level ground and cannot flow upward, in the same way, the Buddha knows exactly how things should abide or should not abide. For example, when someone experiences happiness, the Buddha will know the type of deed the person has done that results in the happiness, and also the type of result that will arise from the deed.

The second power is "knowledge of the law of karma," how certain types of virtuous deeds will have a virtuous result and also how non-virtuous deeds will have a non-virtuous result. He can see specifically the relation of cause and result in each specific case.

The third power is known as "the power of desire." This means that the Buddha knows exactly the desire or intention of every sentient being, whether it be liberation, worldly happiness or wealth.

The fourth power is "the power of the elements." Elements specifically means the race that each person belongs to. The Buddha knows the race or class of every person, whether it be the race of wishing to follow the Hinayana teaching, the race of the Pratiyeka Buddha teaching, or the race of the Bodhisattva or Mahayana teaching.

The fifth power is known as "the power of power." The different qualities of the path such as faith or diligence become power when they are practiced in full. The Buddha knows exactly who has the power of faith, or diligence, and also the level of their faith or diligence, whether they are great or inferior.

The sixth power is "the knowledge of the paths." This means that the Buddha knows all the paths that are known in this world and the corresponding result that will arise through engaging in the paths.

The seventh power is known as "the power of the knowledge of worldly existence and peace," or of samsara and nirvana. This means that the Buddha knows all the different types of samadhi or meditative trances by which one can gain insight into various levels of worldly existence and also the spheres of the different types of enlightenment.

The eighth power is known as "the power of prior births." This means that the Buddha knows not only his previous births but also of all sentient beings, like who they were or what they were in their previous births.

The ninth power is known as "the power of seeing future rebirth." This refers to the Buddha's knowledge of all the aspects of rebirth, like who will die, when they will die, how they will be reborn and where they will be reborn.

The tenth power is known as "the power of knowing how to exhaust the defilements." In other words, the Buddha knows all the methods and teachings there are in order to completely destroy all states of defilements.

The tenth quality of the Buddha is known as "the four states of fearlessness." Here it means that the Buddha is not afraid of proclaiming his own qualities and also the various practices by which others can gain liberation.

The first two states of fearlessness which are in relation to himself mean that the Buddha is able to proclaim to others that he is a completely fully enlightened being. And being able to claim that, he is never afraid that anyone will criticize or debate with him to show that he is not. This is because he has a complete understanding and realization of that state. Also, he is able to claim that he has overcome all the defilements, and has obtained all the perfections of realization such as omniscience. He has no fear of proclaiming it. In contrast to the Buddha, if we were to claim that we are fully enlightened beings, we would be afraid that someone might debate with us to prove us wrong.

The second two states of fearlessness in relation to others means that firstly the Buddha has no fear in telling others that the path leading to worldly existence and suffering is any deed that is based upon the ignorance of grasping at the self. Secondly, he is able to proclaim the path leading to liberation. He is able to say, for example, that through the realization of selflessness of the person and phenomena in this world we are able to gain realization leading to complete liberation and omniscience. And again he is not afraid that anyone is going to blame him because he has complete understanding of the path and how to help others to gain the state of liberation.

The eleventh quality of the Buddha is "the quality of not needing to hide his behavior." Since the Buddha's body, voice and mind are completely purified and enlightened, he has no need to hide the activities of his body, voice and mind from anyone, whereas the ordinary person would try to hide whatever wrong-doing that they have done.

The twelfth quality is known as "the quality of mindfulness or non-forgetfulness." The Buddha does not create any special kind of liking for anyone who listens to his teachings even though that person listens to his teaching properly. Neither does he create any anger toward the person who does not listen to this teaching properly, like falling asleep when he is teaching. This means that the Buddha's mind is always in a state of equanimity so that he has no special liking or dislike for any specific person in this world. Instead, he looks upon everyone with equality.

The thirteenth quality is known as "being free from the defilements along with the residues." Certain lower enlightened beings like the Arhats, for example, though they have destroyed the defilements such as desire, hatred and ignorance, still they have not destroyed the residues of the defilements. This is like when we have gotten rid of something and there is still some little stains remaining behind. When the Arhats gain their form of enlightenment, though they have got rid of the root of all their defilements, still they have not got rid of the residues. Due to that they still have some faults of body and voice. For example, they can walk down the street and by chance step on a snake and be bitten, or they can walk into an elephant that they do not see, or they can be hit by a car while walking on the road, or fall off a cliff when walking along a path.

However, the fully enlightened Buddha, no matter what he is doing, whether he is sitting, standing, walking, or sleeping, at anytime and at any place he has complete omniscience, so that he can never have fault in any of his action of body, voice or mind. At all times and at all places, he has complete knowledge and understanding of every situation and everything that happens in this world. So he can never have any fault like being hit by a car or falling off a cliff.

The fourteenth quality is known as "the state of non-forgetfulness." As ordinary people in this world, we may sometimes forget the time that we are supposed to meet someone, or the action we are going to do next. In the case of the Arhats, sometimes they do forget, as they do not have complete remembrance of every action that they are supposed to do. However, a fully enlightened Buddha knows, for example, exactly where he is supposed to be. There is never any question of forgetting anything. So next time if you have an appointment with the Buddha, you will not have to worry that he will be late.

The fifteenth quality is known as "the quality of compassion." It is said that three times during the day and three times during the night the Buddha looks upon all sentient beings with compassion. This is actually just an example, from the ultimate point of view. The Buddha at all times throughout the day and night looks upon all sentient beings with the eye of compassion. Those who need to be led out of this world of existence or out of the hells or whatever, if the time is ripe or if their conditions are ripe for him to manifest to help them, he will do so. The Buddha is always looking on all these different sentient beings with the eye of compassion in order to lead them through the various paths toward liberation.

The sixteenth quality of the Buddha is known as "the eighteen special qualities which only the Buddha possesses and which no one else in this world possesses." According to the Hinayana tradition, this refers to the eighteen special qualities of the Buddha that we have mentioned, namely the ten powers, the four states of fearlessness, and the three types of remembrance, and great compassion. However, according to the Mahayana, the sixteenth quality constitutes another separate set of eighteen special qualities which the Buddha possesses.

According to the Mahayana, the eighteen special qualities are the six special qualities of behavior, six special qualities of realization, three special qualities of transcendental wisdom and three special qualities of transcendental activities.

Concerning the Six Special Qualities of Behavior

The first one is the behavior of body which is similar to those we have mentioned before such as the Buddha never making a mistake with his body like stepping on a snake or falling off a cliff by accident.

In relation to behavior of his voice, an Arhat for example can shout or laugh in a very improper way. However the Buddha will never make any mistake with his voice as he has complete control and he knows how to use his voice in a proper way.

When an Arhat for example, comes out of meditation, he will perceive the world in a different manner. In a sense, Arhats have two meditative states, one while sitting in meditation and the other when they are out of meditation. The Buddha's mind is always at all times permanently in a state of meditation and he does not alternate between these two states.

The fourth special quality is non-forgetfulness in that whereas the Arhats can forget certain things, the Buddha does not forget anything no matter what situation he is in.

The fifth special quality is the equanimity of mind. When the Arhats see this world of existence, they see it as a state of suffering. It is something which they wish to abandon. When they see nirvana, they see it as a state of happiness which they should obtain. So they have this thought of grasping and relinquishing. The Buddha sees nothing in terms of duality, like good or bad, something to grasp at or something to be relinquished. This state of balance of mind which the Buddha possesses is something that even the other enlightened beings like the Arhats do not have.

The sixth special quality is the Buddha's constant working for the sake of all sentient beings. The Arhats will sometimes examine sentient beings to see if they can help them or not. They do not do it all the time. If they think that they cannot help them, they will leave them alone. They do not always try to help sentient beings. However, the Buddha will at all times examine every sentient being no matter what the circumstance to see if he can help them. If after examination he sees that he cannot help the sentient being, then for the time being the Buddha will not do anything for him because he knows that that person cannot be helped at that time. The conditions are not ripe to help that person. When he sees that there is a need to help them, he will use whatever method is needed. Here the distinction is that the Buddha is always examining all sentient beings in order to help them whereas the other enlightened beings such as the Arhats do not do it at all times.

In relation to the six attainments or six special qualities of realization, this means that the Buddha has six qualities which will never be destroyed. Having achieved the six attainments, he will always be with the six attainments. This refers to his attainment of the truth, his diligence, his wisdom, his state of samadhi, his mindfulness, and also being free from all faults. At all times these will be part of the Buddha's qualities.

The three transcendental wisdoms refer to the Buddha's perfect knowledge of all past, present and future events through his omniscience.

In regard to the three transcendental activities of the body, voice and mind, the Arhats may, through motivation of accomplishing virtue do an activity which, because of the agitation of mind, is transformed into a neutral deed which is neither virtuous nor non-virtuous. It will not be non-virtuous because an Arhat cannot do a non-virtuous deed. It is sort of like a wasted effort and time. However, in the case of the Buddha, all the deeds that he does are always based upon virtue and also result in a virtuous deed. In other words, none of his deeds of body, voice or mind will ever be wasted.

The seventeenth quality of the Buddha is known as "the quality of omniscience." It means that the Buddha is able to answer whatever question that is put to him. In addition, he is able to dispel any doubt of anyone who approaches him.

The eighteenth quality that the Buddha has is known as "the full accomplishments" or the perfect accomplishment of the six perfections. This means that the Buddha has accomplished the six perfections of giving, moral conduct, patience, diligence, meditation and wisdom, and also has completely overcome any obstructing force in relation to these six perfections.

For example, the Buddha has accomplished the entire perfection of giving as well as overcoming any obstructing force to that, such as attachment to the object that he is giving. Or in regard to the accomplishment of the perfection of moral conduct, he does not even have a slight defect in his moral conduct. In this way, the Buddha has accomplished perfectly all the six perfections. Though the Bodhisattvas have accomplished all the six perfections, still they have some slight faults as they have not completely overcome the minor or residual faults which arise.

Fourteen Additional Qualities of the Buddha According to Sakya Pandita

According to the teaching of the Bodhisattva Maitreya in the Mahayanasutralamkara, he said that the Buddha possesses these special eighteen qualities. In addition to these eighteen qualities Sakya Pandita has added another fourteen qualities in the *Sage's Intent.*

The first quality of the Buddha is that "the Buddha has accomplished the benefit of himself and others." This means that through having accomplished the entire path of realization and also the entire path of abandoning all faults, the Buddha is able to perfect his own benefit. He has gained all the various qualities or perfections of enlightenment which anyone in the world is able to gain, and has also destroyed all the non-virtues or defilements. And being able to accomplish his own benefit he is also able to accomplish the benefit of others because he has the qualities of complete omniscience, the power to benefit sentient beings.

The second quality is that "the Buddha has accomplished what is known as the 37 factors or aspects of enlightenment" which are:

The accomplishment of the four states of mindfulness or remembrance. This means looking at the states of the body and mind and to understand that they are empty by nature. Through the state of mindfulness or clarity of mind to see the true nature of mind, body, feeling and perception.

The accomplishment of the four states of pure abandonment. This means that all previous non-virtues have been thoroughly abandoned, that any new non-virtue does not arise within his mind, that all previous virtuous states are increased, and any virtuous state that has not been produced is now produced. So all non-virtue is destroyed and all virtue is increased or developed.

The accomplishment of the four feet or legs of samadhi. This refers to the attainments of certain miraculous powers or abilities which arise from the four different meditative states.

The accomplishment of the five organs like the organs of faith, mindfulness, meditation, wisdom and diligence.

The accomplishment of the five powers. The powers arise when the opposites to the five organs are completely destroyed. For example, when one does not fall under the opposite, such as not having faith in opposition to having faith, and laziness in opposition to diligence.

The accomplishment of the seven branches of the Bodhisattva path which include wisdom and other aspects.

The accomplishment of the Noble Eightfold Path such as right view.

It is said that the Arhats also possess these 37 factors of enlightenment. However, they have not accomplished the factors fully. It is only the perfectly enlightened Buddha who has accomplished these 37 factors completely to their perfection.

The third quality of the Buddha is known as "the possession of all the various states of meditation, the nine states of meditation." This refers to the accomplishment of the four states of meditation found in the form realm, in other words the four dhyanas, and also the four states of meditation in relation to the formless realm. And on top of that, there is also a ninth one which is known as the stainless meditation which means that during that meditative state there is no arising of feeling and also no arising of perception in the mind.

It is said that the Arhats also possess these nine states of meditation. However, in regard to the ninth one, when the Arhat meditates on the ninth stage, he has to do it with very great effort in order to attain that state of meditation. In the case of the Buddha, he does not need any effort. Without any effort the Buddha can spontaneously and effortlessly enter into that meditative state. Also, not only can he enter it without effort, it is also perfectly accomplished whereas the Arhats have to enter it with great difficulty and are still not being able to accomplish it completely.

The fourth quality of the Buddha is known as "the three doors of liberation." This refers to the doors of emptiness, wishlessness and signlessness:

The door of emptiness means that the Buddha, through his meditative state has gained a state free from the duality of grasping a subject and object, to stay in a state of equilibrium between duality.

The door of wishlessness means that the Buddha can relate without attachment to the objects of the senses and also without any desire to be free from them. Generally, when we relate to the objects of the world, there is a grasping after these objects. The Buddha has neither desire for these objects nor to be free from them. It is a state which is devoid of hope and is therefore called the wishless door of liberation.

The door of signlessness means that the Buddha has gained a state of realization which transcends all conceptualization. It is only through concepts or conceptualization that we give names to the things of this world. However, since the Buddha's mind has completely transcended all forms of conceptualization, he does not fall within this state.

It is said that the Arhats have also gained these three doors of liberation. However, they are still involved in some faults in that they have not completely purified themselves with these three meditative states whereas the Buddha has completely gained the state of freedom from any fault.

The fifth quality is known as "the destruction of the four maras:"

The first mara is the mara or demon of the defilements like desire, hatred, ignorance, jealousy and miserliness.

The second mara is the mara of the aggregates like the body and the mind that we have, both of which arise due to the impure defilements, due to grasping at the things in this world. When we have this grasping aggregates like a functioning mind and body which are immersed in the defilements or impure deeds of grasping and the like, then this is known as the state of mara. The Buddha has a body but it is not one which is involved in afflictions anymore. So it means that he has destroyed the mara of the aggregates.

The third mara is the mara of death.

The fourth mara is known as the mara of the heavenly son which is the outer forces or conditions which create obstacles for our dharma path. Especially, there is one heavenly being, one of the kings of heaven who has a great wish to produce in the people's mind great desire for others and also great desire of objects in this world. By creating these obstacles, it throws us off the dharma path.

Through the accomplishment of the transcendental wisdom or knowledge as well as through great compassion, the Buddha has been able to overcome the four maras. Transcendental wisdom means the mind of the Buddha. It is the mind that has been transformed from an ordinary state into the enlightened state at the time of enlightenment. The transcendental wisdom is the realization of ultimate reality, it is the realization of the selflessness of the person as well as the things in this world. This grasping has been destroyed through wisdom which then transforms the mind into a state of transcendental wisdom.

Through gaining this realization of ultimate reality and the state of transcendental wisdom, the various afflictions are destroyed. When we destroy the afflictions of desire, hatred and ignorance, the first mara, the mara of defilements is destroyed. When all the defilements have been destroyed, then it is not possible to take birth anymore because we have gained a state of liberation. When we do not take birth anymore, the aggregates will not arise, which means that the second mara, the mara of aggregates has been destroyed. When one does not take birth anymore then it is impossible to die because when one is not born one does not die. So in this way, the third one, the mara of death has also been destroyed. So these first three, the mara of defilements, of aggregates, and of death are destroyed by the transcendental wisdom which is obtained by the Buddha.

The fourth mara of the heavenly son is destroyed by the Buddha's accomplishment of great compassion. Great compassion itself arises from loving-kindness. The basis of loving-kindness is that everyone in this world is as dear to one as one's own child. Since the Buddha sees through his eyes of great compassion every living being in this world as his only child, then that means that no one can oppose him, that there is no outer force such as the heavenly son which can be perceived as an enemy, as something which can create obstacles. So by transforming that vision of seeing someone who is always making obstacles into someone who is like his only son, into an object of loving-kindness and object of compassion, then that mara of the heavenly son is also destroyed. So in this way, the Buddha overcomes the four maras.

According to the Hinayana tradition, it is said that when the Buddha Shakyamuni attained enlightenment under the Bodhi tree, it was through his meditative state that he destroyed the mara of the afflictions and also the mara of the heavenly son. Later on, in the Buddha's life, at Sravasti when he decided to extend his life for another three months in order to help others though he should have died, it is said that he destroyed the mara of death because he had his own free will to do what he wanted with his own death. Then at the time of his passing away at Kushinagara, since he would never take another physical body of aggregates, he destroyed the mara of the aggregates. So in this way all the four maras were destroyed.

According to the Mahayana tradition however, it is said that at the end of the tenth stage of the Bodhisattva enlightenment, all the four maras along with their subtle residues were completely destroyed. So when one takes the form of a full and perfectly enlightened Buddha there is absolutely no more mara to deal with because they have all been destroyed earlier. So in this way according to the Mahayana, when the Buddha Shakyamuni appeared in this world, he did not have to destroy the maras at that time because they were previously destroyed at the end of the tenth Bhumi.

The sixth quality is known as "the ten powers:"

The first power refers to "the power over life and death." This means that the Buddha is able to stay in this world for as long as he wishes. So he is completely independent of death as he can choose the time when he wants to pass away. There is nothing which can destroy him by accident or at any other time.

The second power is known as "the independence of mind." This means that whereas ordinary people do not have control over their mind, the Buddha has complete control over his mind, to think and to do whatever he wishes to. In this way, he has complete control over his mental states.

The third power is "power of outer forms." This means that the Buddha has the power to appear wherever he wishes or to create any outer form at his free will.

The fourth power is known as "the power over activities or deeds." This means that through the three doors of the body, voice and mind, the Buddha is able to do whatever he wishes. He has complete control and independence of body, voice and mind to accomplish whatever he wishes to do.

The fifth power is known as "the power of birth." This means that the Buddha is able, if he wishes to, take birth anywhere in this world, either as a person, as a god or whatever form that he wishes to take. He has complete control over his birth in this world and also as to how he will appear in this world. For example, whether to appear as a beautiful form or as an ugly form.

The sixth power is known as "the power of desire which means that whatever the Buddha wishes or wants, he can create it." For example, he can turn a piece of earth into gold.

The seventh power is known as "the power of prayer." This means that whatever prayers that the Buddha makes in order to benefit other sentient beings in this world, they will be accomplished.

The eighth power is known as "the power of magic." This means that the Buddha can manifest various forms in order to help sentient beings who are in need of these forms.

The ninth power is known as "the power of transcendental wisdom." This means that the Buddha has accomplished the entire realization of ultimate reality.

The tenth power is known as "the power of dharma." This means that the Buddha is able to teach whatever that is within the three baskets of teaching – moral conduct, sutra and wisdom teaching according to the needs of the listener.

The seventh quality of the Buddha is known as "the quality of various states of samadhi." The states of samadhi can be categorized into two aspects, one which deals with destroying all the faults and one which deals with the accomplishment of all the qualities of realization. Within these two broad categories, there are many different forms of samadhi. For example, the jewel gesture or the mudra of the jewel which refers to accomplishment of various different types of qualities that are able to benefit others, and the vajra-like samadhi which refers to a state of meditation by which all the defilements can be completely destroyed or pacified. In this way, there are many different types of samadhi which the Buddha has accomplished.

The eighth quality is known as "the door of retention." This refers to the quality of retention of mind, of non-forgetfulness. For example, the Buddha has the quality of not forgetting whatever has been said to him. He has a mind which is able to retain everything which is said by anyone to him. Also, it refers to the quality of retaining in his mind all the various aspects of the dharma so that he is able to teach any aspect of the teaching without fear of forgetting or without fear that it will not be presented in a proper way.

The ninth quality is known as "the quality of complete abandonment." The Buddha has abandoned the obscuration of the defilements which blocks liberation and the obscuration of knowable things which block omniscience. There are two aspects of these obscurations. The first is the actual obscuration itself and the other is the residue which comes about after the obscuration has been destroyed. For example, if you place a piece of cloth which has been scented with perfume on the table, there is still some scent remaining behind after the cloth has been taken away. In the same way, even when we have destroyed all the defilements from the root, there is still a slight residue remaining behind. The fully enlightened Buddha has not only destroyed the obscuration of the defilements – desire, hatred and ignorance, and the obscuration of knowable things, but also all the remaining residues.

The tenth quality is known as "the perfection of transcendental wisdom." The transcendental wisdom means the complete perfection of the mind, the mind being transformed into complete knowledge or primordial awareness, or transcendental wisdom. It means that there is no fault and also there is complete realization within the mind of the Buddha. According to the Mahayana there are four types of transcendental wisdom the Buddha has:

The first one is known as "the mirror-like wisdom" or "the wisdom which is mirror-like." This means that all things which can be known in this world the Buddha knows them clearly just like when we see the reflection of something in the mirror, we can see it very clearly. In the same way, every knowable thing in this world is known by the Buddha completely and very clearly.

The second wisdom is known as "the wisdom of equality." This means that the Buddha has completely transcended the state of grasping—subject and object duality. He remains within the non-dual state, that is his mind remains in the state of equilibrium or equality at all times.

The third wisdom is known as "the discriminating wisdom" or "the wisdom of discrimination." As all the qualities of enlightenment arise from the mind, the mind becomes the basis for all the qualities. Since it is the basis for all the qualities of enlightenment, it can discriminate or perceive each one individually. So it is called wisdom of discrimination.

The fourth wisdom is known as "the wisdom of accomplishment." This means that with the perfections that the Buddha has gained, he is able to benefit all sentient beings through whatever means possible. So due to being able to accomplish this, this is known as the wisdom of accomplishment.

The eleventh quality is known as "the quality of speech." This means that the Buddha possesses sixty different qualities of speech. For example, his speech is very gentle, pleasing, without fault, and can be heard from a very long distance. With these qualities of speech he is able through his teaching to bring into the path of liberation gods, man or whoever is suitable to be brought to the state of liberation.

The twelfth quality is known as "the quality of transformation." This refers to the fact that the Buddha has the ability to transform the impure states like the five aggregates, the five sense spheres and the eighteen elements—the six consciousnesses, the six sense organs and the six objects of sense organs into pure states. These are impure because they are based upon the afflictions of desire, hatred and ignorance so that our grasping aggregates are always working in an impure way. However, these five aggregates, five sense spheres and eighteen elements are all transformed by the Buddha into pure states. He is able to function on a very pure level, which means that they are no more involved in any defilement of desire, hatred, or ignorance.

The thirteenth quality of the Buddha is known as "the quality of prosperity." Here it means that the Buddha has prosperity of enlightened qualities such as wisdom, miraculous powers and miraculous emanations. Here the qualities of enlightenment are equated with a state of prosperity. It is said that if we take all the various qualities of prosperity that the worldly person can possibly have, we would think that they are very great.

However, all the qualities of prosperity in this world can be subsumed under one of the many qualities that the Arhat has. Then the many types of prosperity that the Arhat has is subsumed under one of the prosperities of the Pratiyeka Buddha. Then all the many different prosperities that the Pratiyeka Buddha has are subsumed under one of

THE QUALITIES OF THE BUDDHA

the Bodhisattva's types of prosperity. And all the prosperities of the Bodhisattva are subsumed under one prosperity of the fully enlightened Buddha. In this way therefore, the Buddha has many, many forms of prosperity. So in relation to what we think are great prosperities which we can have in this world, they are really insignificant compared to the Buddha's prosperity.

To illustrate the point regarding the quality of prosperity, at one time there was an Arhat by the name of Ubagupta. There was one demon who was trying to obstruct him. The demon went up to Ubagupta and offered him a rosary of flowers which was actually meant to create obstacles for his path. What the Arhat did was to take it and place it around the neck of the demon. Once it was placed around the neck of the demon, it was transformed into the corpse of a dog which was infested with many maggots. No matter how hard the demon tried to take it off he could not do it, and he was very disturbed by it. So then, he promised the Arhat that he would never make any trouble again for anyone on the dharma path, that he will always try to protect them and always promise he would never do anything to harm anyone again. In this way, having made many promises and vows, he was then able to take the rotting corpse off his neck.

This shows that though the qualities which the different demons in this world possess are very powerful, it could be suppressed by just one quality of the Arhat. Just one quality of the Arhat can overcome the qualities or power of anyone of this world.

And to illustrate the difference between the Arhat's and the Bodhisattva's qualities, at one time, Manjushri and

65

Shariputra were traversing the many world systems through their magical power. They went from one world system to another until the end of the three realms of existence. Having gone for a very long distance, Manjushri said to Shariputra that since they had gone so far, they should return through magical means in order to get back quickly. So he asked Shariputra whether he wanted to perform the miracle or whether he wanted him to do it. Shariputra thought that since he had not seen what a Mahayana practitioner could do, he said that they should do it through Manjushri's miraculous power. So Manjushri asked him to close his eyes first. But even before Shariputra could completely shut his eyes, they were right back at the place where they had started. So Shariputra said to Manjushri that his power was very great as they could accomplish such a feat in such a short time. Manjushri said that due to the Arhats' or Hinayana practitioners' lesser degree of faith, their power was much less than that of the Mahayana practitioners.

The fourteenth quality is known as "the Buddha being the most excellent or the highest form of refuge." The reason for this is that the Buddha has completely accomplished all the common and also the uncommon qualities.

Ordinary people of this world are able to gain what is known as the four states of meditative samadhi or dhyana and also the four limitless meditations. This is something which the Buddha has also accomplished. The Arhats are able to gain the different forms of realization such as the 37 factors of enlightenment or the three doors of liberation. This the Buddha too has accomplished. The ten powers like the power over life or the power over the mind which the Bodhisattvas are able to gain, the Buddha has also accomplished. All these are known as the common types of qualities or attainments and the Buddha has all these.

In addition to all these, there are some very special qualities which only the Buddha alone has. These include the eighteen special qualities which no one else has such as the six qualities of behavior, the six qualities of realization, three qualities of transcendental wisdom and three qualities of transcendental activities. In this way, things which other enlightened beings have not been able to accomplish, the Buddha alone has. Since the Buddha has gained all the common and uncommon qualities, he possesses the quality of really being the most excellent and superior refuge. Due to that, he is called the most perfect refuge.

The qualities of the Buddha have been explained in the scriptures in many different ways. According to the Prajnaparamita Sutras it is said that the Buddha's Dharmakaya has 21 qualities and his Rupakaya has 32 major and 80 minor marks. According to the Tantras, the Dharmakaya has 32 qualities and the Rupakaya has 32 qualities. According to the Mahayanasutralamkara of Maitreya it is said that the Buddha has 20 special qualities. According to Sakya Pandita, in addition to those 20 qualities, he added another 14 to describe the various qualities of the Buddha. Actually, some of these qualities of the Buddha are described to enable us to accumulate merit and also in order to produce faith in the Buddha.

In actuality, we are never able to describe every quality that the Buddha possesses because they are really inconceivable and infinite in number. It would be impossible from the basis of the merits that we have to understand the qualities that the Buddha really possesses. So all the qualities we have mentioned are only a partial list of the qualities of an enlightened one.

THE GIFT OF DHARMA TO KUBLAI KHAN

By Choegyal Phakpa

To the incomparable Enlightened One, who is endowed with the splendor of fame in name and the splendor of wondrous virtues in actual fact, I offer homage.

Although you, mighty emperor, know already the discourses on worldly and spiritual science, still, as with the songs and music of musicians to which you listen again and again even when you have heard them all before, why shouldn't a poet repeat wise words?

All of the countless teachings of Dharma taught by the Sage for the sake of countless disciples indeed are meant to be practiced. But how may this be done?

Just as a man bound by fear and shame would not disobey his king's command but dwell in right conduct without harming others and, as a result, would ever grow in good fortune and even earn the praises of his king, so, too, with a person who accepts, in accordance with his ability to accomplish them, the rules of discipline enjoined by the Sage to help beginners on the Hinayana and Mahayana paths: if, after properly receiving vows from an abbot, that person would then guard them because he is bound both by fear of seen and unseen sufferings in worldly existence and by shame whenever he reflects, 'The multitudes of Noble Ones who know the thoughts of other beings will be shamed if I break my vows, . . .'

He, as a result, would become a foundation not only of seen and unseen joys in worldly existence, but of the virtues of perfect liberation; he would also become a worthy object of veneration for men and gods and even receive the praises of Buddhas.

These three realms of existence, after all, are just suffering, while Nirvana, too, is just peace. Looking with pity, therefore, on those who wish either for worldly existence or Nirvana, it is the Buddha alone who, Himself free from sorrow, removes sorrow, and who, having Himself attained great Joy, bestows joy. And He has appeared from amongst beings like ourselves.

The methods He used we can also use. Without timidity and laziness, therefore, you should unwaveringly aspire to win highest enlightenment and feel free to think, 'I must surely attain Buddhahood.' Guard as your own life the vows you have made which, if violated, will cause you to be burnt in hells and which, if preserved, will enable you to experience truly wonderful results in proceeding from joy to joy even now.

Since the three sets of vows—of the Hinayana, Mahayana and Vajrayana paths—are the foundation whereon all virtues may arise, remain and grow within oneself and others, try from the very first to be firm in their observance.

Become certain that the teaching, which is virtuous in its beginning, middle and end, and whose words are quite flawless and not contradictory to the two logical proofs of valid knowledge, is the unique spiritual way among ways.

Know, too, that the Enlightened One who taught it is endowed with unhindered wisdom and great compassion—since He revealed (the truth) without close-fistedness—and also with tremendous power.

Because they are His followers and a gathering of beings with virtues similar to His, because also your own sphere of spiritual activity is identical to theirs, know the Noble Assembly of Bodhisattvas to be the best field for increasing your merit.

Realizing that it is your preceptor who points out and introduces you to these Three Jewels, that he is endowed with the same virtues they have, and that he sustains you with kindliness, always attend and meditate upon him with unflagging faith.

Since they are like yourself in having the nature of being endowed with the causes of pain and with a constant state of unsatisfactoriness, and like yourself, moreover, in wishing themselves to be free from unhappiness and its causes, you should unceasingly meditate great compassion for all living beings.

Recalling the benefits of virtue which you will need in order to attain highest enlightenment and to achieve others' good as well as your own purposes, strive wholeheartedly with genuine devotion to acquire it. In brief, since a mind endowed with faith, compassion and devotion is the precursor of all spiritual accomplishments, perform every least virtue with these three present.

Envision the body of the Enlightened One either in front of you or as your own body, and visualize that your dwelling place is a Buddhafield wherein all beings are Conquerors surrounded by Bodhisattvas and disciples. Then worship yourself and others with oceans of offerings consisting of the enjoyment of the five sense-objects.

Realize that your own virtuous preceptor and all the Conquerors are truly equal and non-dual in form, activity and essential nature. At all times, you should envision him in front of you, or seated atop the crown of your head, or within the lotus of your heart, and pray to him or meditate upon him as being non-dual with yourself.

Of virtue, non-virtue, pleasure, pain and all the phenomena of Samsara and Nirvana, mind is the substratum.

If you were to examine that mind thoroughly from every angle, you would realize that it has neither color nor shape, nor is it single or manifold. It therefore has no nature; therefore it is not arisen, neither does it remain nor cease. It is devoid of both center and periphery, and is thus away from all extremes. It has just the nature of space.

Even so, cognition is not stopped. Hence mind has the nature of non-dual cognition-and-emptiness.

As one's own mind is, so too, is the nature of all beings' minds. Understand thoroughly that all phenomena are non-dual appearance-and-emptiness and place your mind in meditation without grasping.

Through meditating non-dually on the two objects (one's preceptor and the Enlightened One) and objectlessness (emptiness), you will attain a superior meditative state of tranquil concentration (shamatha) which cannot be disturbed by thoughts.

Joyfully remembering that every act of virtue or non-virtue increases the strength of one's virtuous or non-virtuous inclinations, always bring virtues to mind and strengthen them.

Especially should you recollect and analyze the

support, form and experience of your meditation whenever you have meditated upon an object. Through examining further the interdependent origination of their causes and conditions—however many they may be—you will attain meditative insight (vidarshana) through realizing the true state of their suchness, i.e., that no support, form or experience whatsoever exists.

Following the performance of virtues, you should gather together in one all the merit acquired through that (meditation and the like), and fully dedicate them to the attainment of perfect enlightenment by yourself and all these countless beings.

Even though transferable merit may not have been acquired at the time you offer prayers, your wishes nonetheless will be fulfilled if you pray for a great purpose to be achieved—for mind alone is chief. Every virtue which is adorned by this kind of recollection, dedication and noble prayer will increase unceasingly and eventually become the cause of great good for oneself and others.

Everything that is experienced and all other conditioned things (samskrtadharma), i.e. the five aggregates, the senses, sense-objects and sense consciousnesses, are devoid of any nature of their own because they all depend upon causes and conditions.

You should know, therefore, that these external objects also, which appear in various forms to, and are experienced by, mind that is stained by mental impressions, are not real; they are like magical shows which appear due to a variety of causes, they are also like dreams that occur during sleep.

The (so-called) 'unconditioned dharmas'

(asamskrtadharma) are simply ascriptions. A person would have to be mad to wish to propose meaningless names for them, or to indulge in thoughts about them and thereby accept them as 'conditioned dharmas.'

Never scorn the connection between deeds and their results, for (the teachings on) the interdependent origination of cause-and-result as it operates in the sphere of relative truth are not deceptive. You will experience the ripening results of your actions.

There are 'eternalists' in whose view the substantiality of phenomena is accepted. However, no object whatsoever exists which is devoid of (both) direction (i.e., dimension) and time (i.e., consciousness): if you were to analyze the forms of direction and space, you could not possibly find a single entity (which is not reducible to its component parts). And if a 'single entity' does not exist, whence could 'many' appear? As there is no existence other than these, the conceptualization of 'existence' (itself) is an inferior one.

Just as there is no length without shortness, how could a nature of 'nonexistence' be apprehended when even a nature of 'existence' is not obtained?

Know, intelligent one, that the Real also does not consist of 'both' (existence and nonexistence) because this possibility has been removed by the rejection (of each individually); nor does it consist of being 'neither' of the two, because there is no logical proof for this possibility and, in any case, there is no possible 'bothness' to which it could be an alternative.

But if we were to conclude that 'Mind alone is real since it is formless and thus has no directions,' (we would have to admit that) it also becomes plural and false if subject and object are identical, (the latter being manifold).

If, however, subject and object are different to one another, how then do objects become objectified and mind subjectified? If the two arise dually, in what way (e.g., simultaneously or otherwise), do they appear? Finally, what kind of liberation is achieved merely by rejecting illusory external appearances?

Since the object is not established as real by nature, the subject, too, is not established as real. The claim that there exists somehow a pure consciousness apart from these two, is as extremely wrong as the Sankhya philosophers' notion of a 'Self' (purusha) distinct from the transformations of primal nature (prakrter vikara).

Be free from supports, knowing that all phenomena from the first, are un-arisen, natureless, away from extremes and like space.

Marvelous and much more wondrous than any wonder is this knowledge which does not relinquish the emptiness of all dharmas nor yet stop the process of interdependent origination!

Realize that objects are the non-duality of appearance-and-emptiness, that mind is the non-duality of knowledge-and-emptiness, and that the paths to liberation are the non-duality of methods and wisdom. Finally, act (in accord with this insight).

The stages of cause, path and result should be understood thus: the interdependent origination of the relative sphere is like illusion; in the ultimate, the nature of dharmas is emptiness; finally, both are non-dual without differentiation.

Thus, if the foundation (morality), preparation (reflection), meditation, conclusion (dedication of merit and recollection) and the process of practice taken as a whole each be multiplied by three (in correspondence to the three stages of cause, path and result), all the paths of virtue are gathered together in fifteen factors.

Whoever strives to perfect these (fifteen) factors in each performance of virtue enjoys the happiness of fortunate states and accumulates oceans of the Two Collections (merit and transcendent wisdom).

Through the clarity of his meditation, he becomes joined with the Aryan Path and increases in transcendent wisdom as a result of his meditation and noble conduct. Then, attaining the goal (of Buddhahood) through coursing along the final stages of the Path, he puts an end to all thought constructions by realizing the nature of mind to be pure from the very beginning. (His mind) becomes one flavor with the Dharmadhatu and is transformed into the Svabhavikakaya which is the transcendent wisdom of Dharmadhatu and the knowledge of the perfection of renunciation.

For him, the dharmas of worldly existence become transformed through the practice of the path so that his body becomes the Body (of an Enlightened One) adorned by (112) marks and signs of perfection; his voice becomes (the Voice of the Buddha) endowed with sixty tones; his mind is transformed into Transcendent Wisdom and is also endowed with omniscience. Passions are transformed into the boundless virtues of the Conqueror and constitute the Sambhogakaya. His deeds are transformed into the 'Task-Accomplishing Wisdom' and the countless kinds of enlightened activity which form the Nirmanakaya.

These five wisdoms constitute the perfect realization of the Enlightened One and, inasmuch as He is also endowed with spiritual power, they are unending and uninterrupted. May you also, O emperor, become like Him!

Through the merit of offering this gift of Dharma which summarizes the deep sense of the noble path, may all living beings with you, O king, as their chief, quickly attain the highest stage of enlightenment.

My own mind, too, has become encouraged by composing these lines as a gift of doctrine and so I shall speak further of another matter: undistractedly hear it, O Lord among Beings!

The time when you should make efforts is now: make firm the good fortune you have, ensure long life and the success of your lineage and practice right methods to gain liberation.

It is right to make efforts without distraction. At a time when Dharma has not yet set like a sun and a religious king like yourself sits on the throne, how can your mind remain indifferent to the plight of those who wear saffron robes?

Though I am not old, the strength of my body is slight and my mind inclines to be lazy; therefore I wish to be excused for awhile that I may seek Dharma's meaning in solitude.

(Translated by Acharya Lobsang Jamspal and Acharya Manjusiddhartha. Copyright, Victoria Buddhist Dharma Society, 1976).

BUDDHIST TANTRA

By His Holiness Sakya Trizin

There is a common misconception among many non-Buddhists (and even among certain Buddhists) that the Tantras are late and corrupt additions to the Buddha's teachings. This is false. The Tantras are genuine teachings of the Lord Buddha, and they occupy a paramount position within the overall framework of Buddhist doctrine.

Some of the misconceptions about the Tantras stem from their esoteric nature. Since the time of the Buddha the Tantras were always taught secretly and selectively. For their correct understanding they have always required the oral instructions of a qualified master; without such explanations they can easily be misunderstood in wrong and harmful ways. In order to uphold this tradition I too am prevented from discussing most aspects of Tantra here. But it is perhaps permissible here to say a few general things about Buddhist Tantra and about how it is related to other systems of Buddhist and non-Buddhist thought and practice. I shall base myself on the teachings of our tradition such as the *Rgyud sde spyi'i rnam gzhag* ("General System of the Tantras") of Lobpon Sonam Tsemo.

What is Tantra?

In Tibetan tradition the word Tantra (rgyud) normally refers to a special class of the Buddha's teachings like the Kriya, Carya, Yoga and Anuttarayoga Tantras, and more specifically to the scriptures that embody it, such as the Hevajratantra, the Kalacakratantra, and the Guhyasamajatantra. But contrary to its English usage, the word does not usually refer to the whole system of Tantric practice and theory. For the doctrinal system of Tantra the terms Mantrayana ("Mantra Vehicle") and Vajrayana ("Vajra" or "Adamantine Vehicle") are used instead.

In its technical sense the word Tantra means "continuum." In particular, Tantra refers to one's own mind as non-dual Wisdom (jnana); it exists as a continuum because there is an unbroken continuum of mind from beginningless time until the attainment of Buddhahood. This continuum, moreover, has three aspects or stages: the causal continuum, the continuum involved in applied method, and the resultant continuum. Sentient creatures in ordinary cyclic existence (samsara) are the "causal continuum." Those who are engaged in methods of gaining liberation are the "continuum involved in method." And those who have achieved the ultimate spiritual fruit, the Body of Wisdom, are the "resultant continuum." The causal continuum is so called because there exists in it the potential for producing a fruit if the right conditions are met, even though at present that fruit is not actually manifested. It is like a seed kept in a container. "Method" is so called because there exists means or methods by which the result latent in the cause can be brought out. "Method" is like the water and fertilizer needed for growing a plant.

"Fruit" or "result" refers to the actualization of the result that was latent in the cause. This is like the ripened flower that results when one has planted the seed and properly cultivated the plant.

The Place of Tantra in the Buddhist Teachings
In his infinite compassion, wisdom and power the Lord Buddha gave innumerable different teachings aimed at helping countless beings of different mentalities. These teachings can be classified into two main classes: 1) the Sravakayana (which includes the present Theravada), and 2) the Mahayana. The Sravakayana (sometimes also called the Hinayana) is mainly aimed at individual salvation, while the Mahayana stresses the universal ideal of the Bodhisattva ("the Being intent upon the Enlightenment") who selflessly strives for the liberation of all beings, vowing to remain in cyclic existence until all others are liberated. The Mahayana or Great Vehicle can also be divided into two: 1) the Paramitayana ("Perfection Vehicle") which we also call the "Cause Vehicle" because in it the Bodhisattva's moral perfections are cultivated as the causes of future Buddhahood, and 2) the Mantrayana ("Mantra Vehicle"), which is also known as the "Result Vehicle" because through its special practices one realizes the Wisdom of Enlightenment as actually present.

The Spiritual Fruit to be Attained Through Tantra
The spiritual fruit that is aimed at in both branches of Mahayana practice is the Perfect Awakening or Enlightenment of Buddhahood. A Perfectly Awakened Buddha is one who has correctly understood the status of all knowable things in ultimate reality, who possesses

consummate bliss that is free from the impurities, and who has eliminated all stains of the obscurations. The latter characteristic—the freedom from the obscurations—is a cause for other features of Buddhahood. It consists of the elimination of three types of obscurations or impediments: those defilements such as hatred and desire, those that obscure one's knowledge of reality as it is and in its multiplicity, and those that pertain to the meditative attainments.

The Path that Leads to the Fruit
We speak of a method of spiritual practice as a "path" because it is a means by which one reaches the spiritual destination that one is aiming at. There are two types of path, one consists of the common paths that lead to inferior results, and the other is the extraordinary path that leads to the highest goal.

Inferior Paths
Some religious or philosophical traditions while claiming to yield good results actually lead their practitioners to undesirable destinations. For instance, the inferior Tirthikas (non-Buddhist Indian schools) as well as those who propound Nihilism only lead their followers to rebirths in the miserable realms of existence. The higher Tirthikas can lead one to the acquisition of a rebirth in the higher realms, but not to liberation. And even the paths of the Sravakayana and Pratiyekabuddhayana are inferior, for they lead only to liberation, and not to complete Buddhahood.

The Special Path
The special path is the Mahayana. It is superior to both the non-Buddhist paths and the lower Buddhist paths for it

alone is the means by which perfect Buddhahood can be attained. It is superior to all other paths for four particular reasons. It is a better means for removing suffering, it is without attachment to cyclic existence, as a method of liberation it is the vehicle of Buddhahood, and it does not desire only liberation for it is the path of existence and quiescence equally, in which emptiness and compassion are taught as being non-dual.

The Divisions of the Mahayana

The Mahayana itself has two major divisions. As mentioned above, these are the Perfection Vehicle and the Secret-Mantra Vehicle. The first of these is also termed the general Mahayana because it is held in common with both Mahayana divisions, whereas the second is termed the particular because its special profound and vast doctrines are not found within the general tradition. The two vehicles derive their names from the practices predominating within them. In the Perfection Vehicle the practices of the Bodhisattva's perfections (paramita) predominate, and in the Secret-Mantra Vehicle the practices of mantra and related meditations, such as the two stages of Creation and Completion in visualizing the Mandala and the Deity, the mantra recitation and various secret and profound yogas, predominate.

One essential difference between the two Mahayana approaches can be explained by way of their approach to the sensory objects which are the basis for both cyclic existence and Nirvana. In the Perfection Vehicle one tries to banish the five classes of sensory objects outright. One first restrains oneself physically and verbally from overt misdeeds regarding the objects of sense desire, and then through texts and reasoning one learns about their nature. Afterwards through meditative realization one removes all of one's attachment to them. This is done on the surface level through meditatively cultivating the antidotes to the defilements, such as by cultivating love as the antidote to anger, and a view of the repulsiveness of the sense objects as the antidote to desire. And on the ultimate level one removes one's attachment through understanding and meditatively realizing that all of these objects in fact are without any independent self-nature.

In the Mantra Vehicle also one begins by restraining oneself outwardly (the essential basis for one's conduct is the morality of the Pratimoksa and Bodhisattva), but in one's attitude toward the sense objects one does not try to eliminate them directly. Some will of course object that such objects of sensory desire can only act as fetters that prevent one's liberation, and that they must be eliminated. Though this is true for the ordinary individual who lacks skilful methods, for the practitioner who possesses skilful means those very sense objects will help in the attainment of liberation. It is like fire which when out of control can cause great damage, but when used properly and skillfully is very beneficial. While for the lower schools the sense objects arise as the enemies of one's religious practice, here they arise as one's teachers. Moreover, sense objects do not act as fetters by their own natures; rather, one is fettered by the erroneous conceptual thoughts that are based on them.

The Superiority of Vajrayana over Paramitayana
The Secret-Mantra Vehicle is superior to the Perfection Vehicle from several points of view, but its superiority primarily rests in the great efficacy and skillfulness of its

methods. Through Mantrayana practices a person of superior faculties can attain Awakening in a single lifetime. One of middling faculties can attain Awakening in the after-death period (bardo). And one of inferior faculties who observes the commitments will attain enlightenment in seven to sixteen lifetimes. These are much shorter periods than the three "immeasurable" aeons required through the Paramitayana practices. But even though the Mantra Vehicle is thus superior in skilful methods, its view of ultimate reality is identical with the Madhyamika view of the general Mahayana. For both schools the ultimate reality is devoid of all discursive developments or elaborations (nisprapanca). One view cannot be higher than the other since "higher" and "lower" are themselves but discursive developments or conceptualizations.

Preparations and Prerequisites for Tantric Practice

The foregoing has been a general introduction to a few of the basic ideas of Buddhist Tantra. The real question is how to apply these theoretical considerations in useful way, that is, how to practice them. The practice of Mantrayana and further in-depth study of its philosophy requires first of all a special initiation from a qualified master.

Importance of the Guru

One must seek and carefully choose a Guru who has all the qualifications to teach the Tantras: for instance he himself must have received all the necessary initiations and explanations from a qualified Teacher, done long retreats, and learned all the rituals, mudras, drawings of Mandalas, etc. He must also possess great compassion and self-control. In addition to these he may have also received signs of spiritual attainments. It is also very important to find a Guru with whom one has a connection by karma. In any case it is imperative to find a Guru, and one should not practice without a teacher, especially within the Vajrayana. One cannot get any result by merely studying a text. It is said in the Tantras that the Guru is the root and source of all the siddhis and of all realization.

Qualities of the Disciple

Before one can be initiated one will first be examined by the teacher who will ascertain whether one is a fit receptacle for the teachings. The main qualities required are faith, compassion and Bodhicitta (the Enlightenment-Thought). A major empowerment is never given to those who have not developed Bodhicitta to a high degree. In this way both the student and the teacher must examine each other carefully.

Importance of the Transmission

When the right Guru is found, one should then request him for initiation and explanations. In Vajrayana it is necessary to receive the Wang-kur (Empowerment or Initiation), the transmission for permission to practice the Tantra, without which one cannot practice anything. The transmission is particularly important in Vajrayana and the Lama (Guru) assures the continuity of a line of direct transmission through a succession of teachers. This line of transmission has been unbroken since the Lord Shakyamuni Buddha set into motion the Wheel of Dharma. Not only must there be this line of transmission, but also there must be a line of practice, that has kept the lineage alive.

Vows and Practice

After one has been led into the glorious mandala by the master, one begins one's practice, carefully observing the various vows and commitments of the Vajrayana. These vows are primarily mental, and as such they can be even more difficult than those of the Pratimoksa and Bodhisattva systems. One must also devote oneself to further study, and to practicing the specialized visualizations and yogas according to the master's instructions.

Buddhist versus Hindu Tantra
Buddhist Tantra is thus distinguished from the other branches of Mahayana by its special methods. It is, however, identical to the Mahayana Madhyamika in its ultimate view, and it is the same as all Mahayana schools regarding its aim and motivation. Hindu tantra by contrast has different philosophical basis and motivation, even though it shares some of the same practical methodology. Some persons have suggested that Buddhist Tantra must not belong to pure Buddhism because it shares many elements of practice with the Hindus. This is specious reasoning because certain methods are bound to be shared by different religious traditions. Suppose we had to abandon each and every element of practice shared with Hindu traditions. In that case we would have to give up generosity, morality, and much more!

There are of course many further differences between Buddhist and Hindu Tantra in their terminologies, philosophies, and details of their meditative practices, and so forth. But I shall not attempt to explicate them since my own first-hand knowledge is limited to the Buddhist tradition. Here it will be enough to stress that Buddhist Vajrayana presupposes the taking of refuge in the Buddha, Dharma and Sangha (and the Guru as the embodiment of those three), the understanding of Emptiness (shunyata), and the cultivation of love, compassion and Bodhicitta (the Enlightenment-Thought). And I must again underline the importance of Bodhicitta, which is the firm resolve to attain perfect Buddhahood in order to benefit all sentient creature, through one's great wish that they be happy and free from sorrow. These distinguishing features are not found in the non-Buddhist Tantras.

Conclusion

The study of Tantra can only be fruitful if one can apply it through practice, and to do this one must find, serve and carefully follow a qualified master. If one finds one's true teacher and is graced by his blessings one can make swift progress toward the goal, perfect Awakening for the benefit of all creatures. In composing this account I am mindful of my own immeasurable debt of gratitude to my own kind masters. Here I have tried to be true to their teachings and to those of the other great masters of our lineage without divulging that which is forbidden to be taught publicly. I will consider my efforts to have been worthwhile if some harmful misunderstandings have been dispelled. May all beings come to enjoy the true happiness of Buddhahood!

THE SONG GIVEN TO YESHE DORJE

By Jetsun Rinpoche Dragpa Gyaltsen

Namo Guruve.
With folded hands I prostrate
to all the Gurus of the three times.
From my heart, with faith, I go for refuge
to the Sakyapa Jetsun father and son.[1]

Nine limbs are necessary to practice the path
for one possessing faith and the faultless
       precious human birth.
When twelve (limbs) are complete there will
       be Buddhahood
where the two kinds of persons went.[2]
When only explaining the nine limbs,
the Guru, ripening (abhisheka) and samaya-
       three;
hearing, upadesha and diligence-
       three;
place, conducive circumstances and friends-
       three;
at that time, there are nine limbs.

[1.] Jetsun Rinpoche is prostrating to his father, Sachen Kunga Nyingpo, and his brother, Master Sonam Tsemo.
[2.] It is unclear from the text itself who the "two kinds of persons" are, but they may be the persons possessing the aforementioned nine and twelve limbs.

First, when seeking a Guru,
some possess hearing without the upadesha;
(some) possess upadesha without
      knowledge,
while two are complete, (some) have not
      started to practice;
while three are complete, (some) have no
      compassion;
while four are complete, (some) have no diligence.
Having searched and searched for a Guru
      possessing five,
one has delayed and postponed practicing
      the path for a few years,
there is no need to practice as one is not
      ripened-
seek for a sacred Guru to be ripened (by
      abhisheka).
Having arranged and arranged conducive
      circumstances for the ripening (abhisheka),
one has delayed and postponed practicing
      the path for a few years-
without protecting samaya,[3] there is no
      result.
When there is no hearing there is no wisdom;
when there is no upadesha, there is no
      essence;
having arranged and arranged those three
      conducive circumstances,
one has delayed and postponed practicing
      the path for a few years,

[3.] Samaya is the Vajrayana vow.

but the previous delays were not useless.
The three conducive circumstances for
        oneself are complete.
To meet the nine kinds of necessary limbs,
now, having urged (you) with the whip of
        diligence,
please do not be lazy in practice.
Because one wishes to practice the path, find
        a secluded place-
thieves may come if one resides in seclusion.
One is carried away by distractions in the
        middle of an assembly.
Having thought and thought where to stay,
do not let (oneself) be exhausted in making
        preparations.
Having gathered all the necessities of
staying in seclusion, seek seclusion.
Also where ever one stays, give up
        distraction.
Do not neglect emphasis on practice!
When necessities are many, distraction is
        great;
when necessities are few, conducive
        circumstances are poor.
Having thought and thought of these two,
to practice the path, do not engage in
        laziness!
When the necessities exist, gather the
        accumulation (of merit);
although the various necessities are not
        gathered,

whatever necessities one has, should be used
      for food and clothing.
Tame one's mind with humble conduct,
but humble conduct can become meaningless
      words.
When one has many friends, one will be
      carried away by the obstacle of distraction;
even between friends, conversation is an
      obstacle.
Simply remain, not hearing pleasant
      conversations,
with persons who are in accord with Dharma.
If one does not meet with a friend like that,
remain in solitude to tame one's mind.
To complete the twelve harmonious limbs-
abandon all the faults of disharmonious
      circumstances;
now, do not stay under the influence of
      laziness!
I request you to emphasize practice.
When one wishes to practice, remain relaxed!
Having arranged conducive circumstances,
      remain relaxed;
having been fatigued by listening and
      contemplation, remain relaxed;
having contemplated on any object at all,
      remain relaxed.
Without a day job, observe the object;
thinking was done because one possesses
      activities.
Recall the qualities of samsara's defilements;

the qualities are to be explained here-
enthusiasm develops by looking at form,
possessing many shapes and colors,
with the ordinary unobscured eye;
joy is developed having looked inwardly.
Astonishment develops because various
       sounds are heard
with the ordinary unobstructed ear;
wisdom increases because various speech is
       heard,
enthusiasm develops by engaging in various
       conversations.
The amazing objects of smell and taste are
       consumed
with the unobstructed ordinary nose and
       tongue;
an astonishing variety of experiences arise;
giving to others develops enthusiasm.
Enthusiasm develops by (contacting) many
       faultless tangibles
with the ordinary body organ[4] without
       disease,
and also (tangibles) are given to others;
further, other minds will develop enthusiasm.
With virtuous thinking
the various qualities of the three times
       develop-
wisdom increases and one becomes
       enthusiastic.

---

4. The body organ is the basis of the sense of touch and pervades the entire body.

The sun having set, remaining in bed,
not sleeping, thoughts come and go.
The thoughts thought during the day come
    from delusion-
recall the faults of samsara at night.
Satisfaction by consuming objects is never
    seen;
although satisfied, also essence is never seen.
Possessing the essenseless essence,
the desiring thought to consume objects is pitiful.
Having consumed and consumed
    unsatisfactory objects,
one cannot even guess where all the days have
    gone.
Having accomplished and accomplished an
    unsatisfactory objective,
one cannot even guess where all the months
    and years have gone.
Searching for the essenceless essence,
investigating the purposeless objective,
having been distracted and distracted by
    meaningless chaff,
one will not perceive changing things.
One's head is held by fangs of white hair;
furrows of wrinkles are drawn on the skin;
one is left with gums, without any teeth in
    the mouth;
one relies on a cane without any strength in
    the body;
one is disrespected by all young adults;
death closely approaches the elderly body;
although elderly, still one possesses the

thought of permanence.
Not dying in youth, one's great expectations
     are godlike.
Because it does not matter whether one is
     young or old,
one is afflicted by the birth and death of
     imbalanced elements.
One's guardian gods[5] leave for elsewhere,
harmful ghosts and spirits arrive in one's
     presence.
The body is without strength, depending on
     others.
One is contorted (with pain) because of
     eating and drinking,
one is harmed by many sufferings in the
     body.
One cries out if there are relatives.
One is greatly harmed by Yama, the lord of
     death.[6]
One leaves the appearances of this world;
also, there is no boundary limiting where one
     will go.
All places are pervaded by great darkness.
One is driven from behind by
     Karmayamas;[7]
also, one hears the sounds of terrifying lower
     realms.
At that time, if merit is one's protection,

---

5. Guardian gods are those with whom one will make a relationship with to protect oneself.
6. According to Vasubandhu's Abhidharmakosha-bhashyam, Yama is the king of the preta realm.
7. The servants of yama who drive beings into the hot hells and torture them.

also, there is no (merit accumulated) to rely
    upon.
Also, by consuming objects in the past
much harm without benefit occurred.
Because the faults of samsara were not
    contemplated,
alas! One's mind was left in an inferior state.
At daybreak, remaining in solitude in a
    secluded place,
thinking intensely of yesterday's faults of
    samsara
up and down, again and again,
the wish for the place of liberation will arise.
By considering what will achieve that,
if the three- wisdom, method and conduct-
were contemplated well, one may be
    liberated.
In the beginning, the view of wisdom arises.
As before, the thoughts of the day are
    deluded;
possessing an amazing array of various
    objects,
by observing the amazing (object),
having seen the essenceless essence,
one discovers the essence of the ultimate
    meaning.
One cannot find objects by observation-
it is best to leave those essenceless (objects).
One cannot find form by observation-
leave (the mind) relaxed in a state of not
    finding form.

The appearance of form is similar to a
　　　　reflection in a mirror-
it is best to leave (the appearance of form)
　　　　like an illusion.
One cannot find sound by hearing-
every sound is similar to an echo.
Having examined non-arising sound-
leave (the mind) relaxed in the state of an
　　　　echo.
Smelling, touching and tasting- three,
if objects are seen arising and ceasing,
the experience of appearances are just
　　　　reflections-
leave (the mind) relaxed in the state of
　　　　awareness and emptiness.
That cause of thought is not discovered by
　　　　the thinking mind,
because the arising and ceasing of whatever is
　　　　thought is also not discovered;
that without center or periphery is like space-
leave (the mind) relaxed in the state of
　　　　non-arising.
There are no higher or lower objects at all;
there is no arising or ceasing at all;
there is no good or bad at all-
leave (the mind) in the state of the equality
　　　　of dharmas.
The thoughts thought yesterday are
　　　　deluded;
non-arising was thought to be arising;
freedom from illness and aging was thought
　　　　(to be illness and aging);

non-cessation was thought to be cessation;
because in the beginning, dharmas did not
        arise-
where is abiding or cessation possible?
Because the thought of non-arising and
        non-ceasing
increases conceptuality- leave (it) and go!
Even leave one's leaving and go!
Even one's leaving is conceptual.
Having no comprehension of spontaneous
        reality,
because the oral instruction of non-grasping
        was not cultivated,
even whatever one thought became grasping;
also, the thought of non-grasping became
        grasping.
Clarity is unceasingly selfless-
may the reality of union be comprehended.
That one-pointed activity of meditation
is in the hand of those possessing diligence.
Without sending (meditation) to the
        enemy- sluggishness and agitation,
practice the path of calm-abiding and
        insight.
To practice (calm-abiding and insight), the
        profound oral instructions
are in the tantra divisions of Vajrayana.
Because Vajrayana cannot be sung in song,
I have to keep the upadeshas in my mind.
For one who wishes to perform conduct,
the seven kinds of individual liberation

vows[8]
are an ornament for Bodhisattvas.
By developing earnestness in practicing those,
there will be no wild conduct of body and
        speech.
Not contradicting Buddha's teaching,
one does not cast demeaning harsh words at
        living beings;
one is not distracted to the ordinary;
because these are very beneficial qualities-
        develop earnestness.
Because this is the root, do not be lazy.
For the person who possesses that basis,
there are three kinds of Vajrayana conduct-
leave that elaborate (conduct) difficult to
        acquire,
see what is accomplished by either the
        un-elaborate or
the very un-elaborate (conduct), and develop
        earnestness.
If one practices according to these words,
Buddhahood will be in one's hand;
it will not be long before it is in one's hand,
the result will be accomplished without
        difficulty.
On the western side of Palden Sakya
        mountain,
when just going there with desire to entertain
        the senses,
the one possessing faith, Yeshe Dorje,

---

8. The seven kinds of individual liberation vows are of the monk, nun, male novice, female novice, male layperson, female layperson and the fast day vow holder.

      arrived,
and asked me to write meaningful verses
without contradicting the meaning of
      reality,
and if contemplated will arouse realization.
Rigzin Dragpa was brought along- he was
      asked to take dictation.
If read on occasion, realization will arise;
if contemplated, it is beneficial to the mind-
this may be of benefit to others.
Sing mounted on the steed of song;
be blessed like the Great Jetsun.
By the virtue of this writing, whatever is
      obtained by me, by that,
may all of however many sentient beings
      pervade space
quickly obtain highest complete Buddhahood.

INSTRUCTIONS ON PARTING FROM THE FOUR ATTACHMENTS

By Jetsun Rinpoche Dragpa Gyaltsen

From my heart I go for refuge;
to the kind Gurus
and the compassionate Yidam[9] deities,
please bestow blessings upon me.
There is no need for non-spiritual activities;
to practice according to Dharma,
I will bestow the oral instruction of Parting
    from the Four Attachments,
and give it for you to hear.

The offering salutation and the resolution to explain.
When attached to this life, one is not a spiritual
    person.
When attached to samsara,[10] one has no
    renunciation.
When attached to one's own benefit, one has
    no bodhicitta,[11]
When grasping occurs, one does not have the
    view,[12]
First, (practice) discipline, and hearing,
    contemplation and meditation,

---

9. Yidams are the deities one is committed to in Vajrayana spiritual practice.
10. Samsara is the cycle of rebirths through the desire, form and formless realms.
11. Bodhicitta is the aspiration to achieve Buddhahood for the benefit of sentient beings.
12. View here refers to the correct view of freedom from proliferation.

without attachment to this life;
such practice having an objective for this life,
is not a spiritual person's, leave it aside.
In the beginning, when only discipline[13] was
     explained-
with the root of accomplishing higher
     realms,[14]
with the staircase of accomplishing
     liberation,[15]
with the antidote of abandoning suffering-
although there is no method without such
     discipline;
yet such discipline attached to this life-
with the root of accomplishing the eight
     worldly dharmas,[16]
with harsh words for inferior discipline,
with jealousy toward those who maintain
     discipline,
with wild conduct in one's own discipline,
with seeds of accomplishing lower realms-[17]
leave such pretentious discipline aside!
That person doing hearing and
     contemplation-
with the wealth of accomplishing what is to
     be known,
with the lamp which removes ignorance,
with understanding of the path of guiding

---

13. Discipline is the vows Buddhists hold as the basis for practice.

14 Human realm, titan realm and god realm.

15 Liberation is the cessation of suffering.

16 The eight worldly dharmas are loss and gain, notoriety and fame, praise and blame, pleasure and pain.

17 Lower realms are animal, preta and hell realms.

living beings,
with the seed of Dharmakaya-[18]
although there is no method without such
          hearing and contemplation;
yet such hearing and contemplation attached
          to this life-
with the wealth of accomplishing pride,
with contempt for inferior hearing and
          contemplation,
with jealousy for those who have hearing and
          contemplation,
with the quest for wealth and followers,
with the root of accomplishing realms-
leave such hearing and contemplation of the
          eight worldly dharmas aside!
All persons doing meditation-
with the antidote of abandoning
          defilement,[19]
with the root of accomplishing the liberating
          path,[20]
with the wealth of comprehending reality,
with the seed of accomplishing Buddhahood-
although there is no method without such
          meditation;
yet such a meditation focused on this life-
with preoccupation even when staying in a
          solitary place,
with recitation of pointless conversation,

[18.] Dharmakaya is the luminous clear empty nature of the mind realized by Buddhas.

[19] The three root defilements are desire, anger, and ignorance.

[20] There are five paths; the paths of accumulation, application, seeing, cultivation, and no more learning.

with scorn for those doing hearing and
        contemplation,
with jealousy towards other meditators,
with complete distraction in one's own
        meditation-
leave such concentration meditation of the
        eight worldly Dharmas aside!

These (stanzas) above refer to the meaning taught in the
Abhidharmakosa; "Abiding in discipline, possessing
hearing and contemplation (it is) always applied to
meditation," which directly demonstrates the distinction
between the true and the false. The method of meditating
the difficulty of obtaining the precious human birth, and
impermanence and death are demonstrated indirectly.

In accomplishing nirvana-
please also abandon attachment to the three
        realms;
to abandon attachment to the three realms,
please recall the faults of samsara.
First, that suffering of suffering
is the suffering of the three lower realms.
One will shiver if that is well contemplated;
if that falls on oneself, it cannot be endured.
As the virtue of abandoning will not be
        accomplished,
one cultivates lower realms;
also that is where the pitiful one exists.
When only contemplating the suffering of
        change-
the higher are born in lower realms;

Sakra[21] is born as an ordinary being;
the sun and moon are darkened by an
      eclipse;
a Cakravartin king[22] is born as a subject.
Although one can be convinced about that
      depending on scripture,
because it is not possible for the ordinary to
      comprehend those (examples);
look at the changes of people visible to
      oneself.
Rich people become homeless;
powerful voices become weak;
many people become one person;[23]
those (changing conditions), etc., are
      inconceivable.
When only contemplating the suffering of
      the conditioned-
there is no end to the activities to be done.
Although suffering (exists) for many people,
      also suffering (exists) for a few;
although suffering (exists) for the wealthy,
      also suffering (exists) for the hungry.
All human lives are exhausted in
      preparations;
although one dies, there is no end to
      preparations.
Entering the start of the preparations of the
      next life,[24]

---

21. Sakra is the king of the gods of the thirty three heavens.
22 A king whose sovereignty is symbolized with a wheel.
23 This can refer to a large family dwindling down to one member, etc.
24 These 'preparations' refer to the unending activities of the next life.

the pitiful one creates attachment
to the aggregated suffering of samsara.
By these (stanzas) above, having directly demonstrated
the faults of samsara, the acceptance and rejection of
cause and result are indirectly demonstrated.

When parted from attachment, one goes to
            nirvana;
when gone to nirvana, one obtains bliss;
this is the song of experience of freedom
            from the four attachments.
By liberating myself alone, there is no benefit
            for
my parents, the sentient beings of the three
            realms;
one's parents are left in the thicket of
            suffering;
one who desires his own happiness is pitiful.
May the suffering of the three realms ripen
            on me;
may sentient beings take my merit,
by the blessing of this merit
may all sentient beings become Buddhas.
By these (stanzas) above, the cause, meditating loving-
kindness and compassion, is demonstrated indirectly,
having directly demonstrated the result, exchanging self
and other.

Further, however I remain with grasping,
in the state of dharmata[25] there is no

---

25 The nature of things.

liberation.
Further, when only that is precisely
      explained-
there is no liberation when grasping to
      existence;
there is no higher realm when grasping to
      non-existence;
because grasping to both is not known-
it is best to leave (the mind) in a state of
      non-duality.
By the (stanzas) above, having abandoned the view of
permanence and annihilation, in general, the way to place
the mind in non-dual union is demonstrated.

All dharmas are objects of mind's activity;
without searching for a creator of the four
      elements,
luck, God, etc.-
it is best to leave (mind) in the state of
      mind itself.
By the (stanzas) above, having demonstrated the stages of
the path in common with the Mind Only Bodhisattva's
school, the uncommon Mahayana Madhyamika follows;

The nature of appearances as illusion,
and dependent origination's
reality cannot be known to be expressed-
it is best to leave (mind) in the state of
      inexpressibility.
By these (stanzas) above, having demonstrated indirectly
how to meditate calm-abiding, in the method of

meditating insight, establishing appearing objects as mind, establishing that (mind) as illusion, establishing that (illusion) as being without self-nature, and having determined dependent origination and inexpressibility, the meditation of union free from proliferation is directly demonstrated.

Having explained *Parting from the Four Attachments*,
by the merit of this virtue,
may all the seven kinds of living beings be
established on the stage of Buddhahood!
By these (stanzas), the dedication and result are demonstrated.

The Instruction on *Parting from the Four Attachments* was composed by the Yogin Dragpa Gyaltsen at Palden Sakya[26] Monastery.

---

26. Palden Sakya is in the Western region province of Tibet where the Sakya order was established.

The Verse Instruction on How to Guide Students According to the Treatises of the Path and Result

By Jetsun Rinpoche Dragpa Gyaltsen

I prostrate to the assembly of Glorious
   Gurus,
Secondly, I bow to Vajradhara,
listen to this explanation with few words,
the essential meaning of all the Sutras,
   Tantras and Treatises.

The suffering of suffering is in the places of
   the three lower realms,
like cuts on top of leprous sores;
if it is contemplated well, how will one be
   able to endure it?
That thought turns one away from
   non-virtuous deeds.

Also, in three higher realms, there is [the
   suffering of] change and the conditioned.
First, one should think that the high becomes
   low;
second, how will activities be completed?
Therefore, first, contemplate the faults of
   samsara.

Having stayed in a secluded place, to
      meditate dhyana,
if one is friends with childish beings, because
      one will not obtain seclusion,
meditate detachment toward those beings;
by this seclusion is obtained and wrong
      livelihood is abandoned.

In that way, having left worldly concepts,
go for refuge to the Three Jewels;
meditate the bodhichitta of equalizing and
      exchanging self and others;
and also utlimate bodhichitta.

Also contemplating in that way, if there is
      craving for this life,
in between all sessions recall impermanence
again and again, because it is useless
to pass the time without always thinking of
      impermanence.

In between sessions of meditating the two
      bodhichittas
be diligent in reading sutras and making
      offerings to the Three Jewels.
Having condensed the treatises of the
      perfection vehicle,
these are the upadeshas of the essential meaning.

If one's intelligence is not fulfilled by just
      that,

those of greater intelligence should be
      interested in the profound learning;
whoever wishes to quickly obtain [the stage
      of] Mahavajradhara,
should be given the Vajrayana.

Rely closely on the Guru with lineage and
      knowledge of the meaning of the Tantras,
supremely protecting samaya, ornamented
      by many upadeshas,
moistening the continuum with compassion,
      knowledgeable in many treatises,
and make many requests.

Enter into the great mandala when it is
      granted by them
to obtain the four abhishekas completely;
not by just the brief blessings,
because the root of Vajrayana is abhisheka.

After that, earnestly train in the
root together with the branch samayas;
also just with those, in sixteen births,
there will be accomplishment—[samaya] is
  the basis of all paths.

In that way, having demonstrated the
      creation stage together with the branches
to a person who is a suitable recipient,
purifying the continuum by the mantra
      recitation and fire puja;

after that one does the mind training in the
      perfect view.

First, all things are established as mind;
there is nothing else here not included in
      mind;
having one's mind contaminated by the
      traces of delusion,
is like a dream horse or ox, or a fault of
      vision.

That mind is an illusion without essence,
like a mirage, moon in water, fire from
      friction;
merely appearing from the assembly of
      various conditions,
this describes what the nature of the mind is.

The essence of what is called "illusion"
does not exist here, it dependently
      originates;
if there is no arising, ceasing or abiding,
in this inexpressibility, what is to be
      thought?

Here, because expressing the inexpressible is
      meaningless,
and there is no basis of thinking the
      unthinkable;
in this non-meditation what is to be
      meditated?

If understood in that way, there will be no
        grasping.

Having trained the mind by contemplating
        the perfect view,
after that, one should meditate the
        concentration of the two stages;
training the mind gradually in the creation
        stage,
both mind and awareness hold that as a
        support.

First, in the creation stage itself,[27]
until obtaining the appearance [of the deity
        mandala] with[28] mind;[29]
second, the complete mandala or
        simultaneously arising;[30]
having done whichever preliminary,[31]
        meditate the completion stage.

The preliminaries for all the profound
        completions are
the three kinds of purification,[32] after that
        training in the air;[33]
the seven exercises, the main one, the
        vase exercise;

---

27. The practice connected to the vase abhiseka.

28. Pomar, yis; Sakyakabhum, yi.

29. The gradual creation of the deity mandala by mind.

30. The instant creation of the deity mandala through mere awareness.

31. The two methods of creation given above.

32 Mandala offerings, Vajrasattva recitation and Guruyoga.

33 Pranayama.

the path of the Buddhas is based on the pure
vase exercise.[34]

This is the elixir of deathlessness,
this is supreme medicine against aging,
also this accomplishes many
powers,
also this stabilizes the dependent
origination of the two stages.

Self blessing, inner heat and the subtle drops,
three,
both the actual karmamudra and the
jnanamudra,
in that way, also the two kinds of completion
stage,
demonstrates how to train in the preliminary
training.

All the profound upadeshas separate from
the vase exercise,
are paths of gradual accomplishment;
because [they] do not accomplish [the path]
quickly,
for that reason, have devotion to the path of
the vase exercise.

The qualities of Buddhahood are placed on
the hand of the vase exercise;
practitioners of meditating the vase exercise,

[34.] Refers to air yoga of retention

first, for a long time be diligent in physical
      exercises,
having aroused experience, mix with view.

From the beginning, one's mind, the cause
      continuum free from proliferation,
the view of the path of the wisdom of the
      abhisheka,
the experiences and the stage of
      Buddhahood are essentially the same;
the special realizations are demonstrated by
      the examples of the moon.

Some say "mahamudra descends from
      above;"
some ignorant teachers in the past have said
      that;
that is not mahamudra, it is view of
      dhyana;
mahamudra is produced by the force of the
      meditation.

In that way, by meditating the path of the
      two stages,
having obtained heat, stabilized by conduct,
having accomplished the stages, connected
      by the application of the near causes,
the real stage of Vajradhara will be
      obtained.
Traton Lodro with faith and devotion,
interested in the essential meaning without

details,
requested the lay yogin Dragpa Gyalsten
to compose this at Sakya.

Having taken the essence of the essential to
          teach this,
by the merit produced from writing well
these twenty seven verses and this eighth,
may all living beings progress to the stage of
          a vajra holder.

I confess the assembly of faults before the
          Gurus and the Buddhas,
and dedicate the virtue to all sentient beings,
          may obstacles be pacified.

Biographies of the Authors

PETER DELLA SANTINA

Peter Della Santina was born in the USA. He has spent many years studying and teaching in South and East Asia. He received his B.A. in Religion in 1972 from Wesleyan University, Middletown, Connecticut, and his M.A. in Philosophy from the University of Delhi, India in 1974. He earned his Ph.D. in Buddhist Studies also from the University of Delhi, India in 1979.

He spent three years at the Institute for Advanced Studies of World Religions, Fort Lee, New Jersey, as a research scholar translating 8th Century Buddhist philosophical texts from Tibetan into English. He taught at several universities and Buddhist centers in Europe and Asia including the University of Pisa in Italy, the National University of Singapore, and Tibet House in Delhi, India. He was the Coordinator of the Buddhist Studies Project at the Curriculum Development Institute of Singapore, a department of the Ministry of Education, from 1983 to 1985.

More recently, he held the position of Senior Fellow at the Indian Institute of Advanced Studies, Simla, India and taught Philosophy at the Fo Kuang Shan Academy of Chinese Buddhism, Kaoh-shiung, Taiwan.

For 25 years, Peter Della Santina has been a student of His Holiness Sakya Trizin, leader of the Sakya

Order of Tibetan Buddhism and of other eminent abbots of the Sakya tradition. He has practiced Buddhist meditation and has completed a number of retreats.

He has published several books and articles in academic journals including "Nagarjuna's Letter to King Gautamiputra," Delhi 1978 and 1982, "Madhyamaka Schools in India," Delhi 1986, and "Madhyamaka and Modern Western Philosophy," Philosophy East and West, Hawaii, 1986.

KHENPO APPEY RINPOCHE

Venerable Khenpo Appey Rinpoche received his early monastic training and education in the province of Kham in Eastern Tibet, where he was born. Later he moved to the Ngor Monastery in Central Tibet. He has performed many retreats and given many teachings and initiations. He was abbot of Dzongsar University in Eastern Tibet before fleeing to India.

He fled Tibet during the communist invasion and has since been residing in India where, until 1967, he was tutor to His Holiness Sakya Trizin. Together with His Holiness Sakya Trizin, they were the main motivating forces behind the founding of the Sakya College of Buddhist Philosophy in 1972 in Mussoorie, India, where he served as principal and taught for many years until moving to Nepal to start another Sakya College in Boudhanath, Nepal.

CHOEGYAL PHAGPA

Choegyal Phapga [1235-1280 A.D.], was the fifth founding master of the Sakya Order of Tibetan Buddhism. His father was Zangtsa Sonam Gyaltsen and his mother was Machig Kunkyi. From the very early age of three Chogyal Phapgpa began giving teachings. Scholars were amazed at his knowledge at such a young age, and called him Phagpa, or the Noble One. He received the monk's vow in front of Jowo Shakyamuni's shrine in Lhasa from his uncle Sakya Pandita when he was ten years old.

At seventeen, Choegyal Phagpa traveled to Mongolia with Sakya Pandita and studied general Buddhist subjects and many Tantric teachings with him. Before passing away, Sakya Pandita presented him with a white dharma conch which symbolizes the spreading of dharma both far and near, and a monk's bowl symbolizing the establishment of monastic traditions. Sakya Pandita asked him to help others by recollecting his past vows and resolutions. Choegyal Phagpa arranged an elaborate funeral for Sakya Pandita.

At nineteen, the great Mongolian king Kublai Khan invited Choegyal Phagpa to give the Hevajra initiation to a group of twenty-five royal members and introduced them to Vajrayana Buddhism. In return, the king offered him a portion of Tibet, which was then under Mongolian control, and proclaimed Choegyal Phagpa as "Tishri." After this, Sakyas became the spiritual and temporal rulers of Tibet and Choegyal Phagpa became the first monk or Lama in history to rule Tibet.

He received full ordination from Abbot Nyethangpa Dakpa Senge when he was twenty-one years old and studied several Buddhist subjects under his guidance. When Choegyal Phagpa was twenty-three he invited Thongton to "Five Peak Mountains" of China to receive many teachings. At that time he also visited royal courts and while giving teachings, defeated seventeen heretics. When he was thirty years old, Choegyal Phagpa returned to Sakya and bestowed many teachings there. He invited many masters and received more teachings and became the great master of dharma. Again, at the age of thirty-three, at the invitation of the king, he traveled to China and assigned the responsibilities in Tibet to thirteen deputies. As an offering of gratitude for bestowing initiations, the king bestowed many offerings to Choegyal Phagpa and to the people of Tibet. All the offerings were used in the service of the dharma for constructing and financing religious artifacts, and toward the welfare of monks and poor people.

In this way, Choegyal Phagpa spread the dharma in Tibet, China and Mongolia and became Abbot of 400,000 monks. He gave teachings in many languages and benefited many people. Further, he composed many texts of commentaries, practical instructions and questions and answers. At forty-six Choegyal Phagpa passed away.

HIS HOLINESS SAKYA TRIZIN

His Holiness Sakya Trizin was born in Tsedong near Shigatse (South Tibet) on the first of the eighth Tibetan month (September 7, 1945). "Sakya Trizin" means "The Throneholder of Sakya." His Holiness is the 41st Patriarch of the Sakya Sect, one of the four main sects of Tibetan Buddhism, and is a direct descendent of the Khon Lineage, a very ancient Tibetan religious family that according to legend had heavenly origins.

His formal studies started at the age of five, although even before that he had received several empowerments from his own father. In fact, he received his first empowerment, one of long life, as soon as he was born.

In the course of intensive studies at Sakya, Ngor, Lhasa, and later in India, he received all the major transmissions of the Sakya Lineage such as the exoteric and esoteric *Lam Dre* (Path containing its Result) Teachings, the *Drubthab-Kundu* (a collection of Tantric empowerments and practices), the Vajrayogini instructions, the *Zhenpa Zhidral*, etc. From a tender age he memorized many texts, like the *Hevajratantra*, performed many retreats and gave numerous empowerments. He also received many teaching from the other traditions of Tibetan Buddhism.

His main Gurus were the Ngor Abbots Ngawang Lodro Shenpen Nyingpo, Khangsar Shabdrung, Lama Ngawang Lodro Rinchen, the Venerable Jamyang Kyhentse Rinpoche, the great Nyingmapa yogi Drupchen Rinpoche, Phende Khenpo, Sakya Khenpo Jampal Sangpo, His father, Dezhung Rinpoche and Chogye Rinpoche.

He formally acceded to the Throne of Sakya in early 1959. Almost immediately after the coronation ceremony, he had to leave for India because of the Chinese Communist takeover of Tibet. He stayed first in Sikkim, where he started to learn English, then in Darjeeling where he spent three years mastering philosophical studies under Khenpo Rinchen. Finally, he went to Mussoorie, and in March 1964, founded the Sakya Centre in Rajpur, Dehra Dun. At that time he studied intensively the Tantras and received many profound explanations from Khenpo Appey until 1967. He also continued his studies of English. From 1971 to 1972 he received the *Gyude Kundu*, a major collection of Tantras, from the Venerable Chogye Trichen Rinpoche.

At the age of 22, he gave the *Lam Dre* Teaching for the first time to a large gathering at Sarnath, Varanasi. In the same year he also inaugurated the Sakya rehabilitation settlement at Puruwala in Himachal Pradesh, 40 miles from Dehra Dun.

His Holiness gave the *Drubthab-Kundu* to a large assembly in Ladakh in 1976. Since then, he has given *Lam Dre* teachings numerous times all over the world. In 1981, His Holiness inaugurated the new temple at Puruwala which is now the Seat of the Sakya Order.

His Holiness has been ceaselessly serving the Dharma. He has many disciples in India and other countries, and has made several journeys to the West where he has taught extensively and founded many dharmas centers.

JETSUN RINPOCHE DRAGPA GYALTSEN

Jetsun Rinpoche Dragpa Gyaltsen [1147-1216 A.D.], the third of the three lay Founder Masters, was born in the fire rabbit year to Sachen Kunga Nyingpo and Jomo Machig Od-dron. As a young child Jetsun Rinpoche delighted in solitude, was free from mundane desires, diligent in practicing virtuous qualities and was free from childish conduct.

He received lay vows from Bodhisattva Dawa Gyaltsen when he was eight years old. His conduct was more disciplined than that of the monks. He never touched meat or alcohol apart from the meat and alcohol used as samaya substances in the ganachakra feast offering.

His principal Gurus were his father Sachen, and his elder brother, Master Sonam Tsemo. He also received many teachings of the three baskets and four tantra divisions from numerous Tibetan, Indian and Nepalese masters, such as Nyan Tsugtor Gyalpo, Zhang Tsultrim Drag, Nyag Wang Gyal, Jayasena, the translator Pachog Dangpo Dorje and the yogi Avadhutipa, etc.

Jetsun Rinpoche began teaching at eleven years of age, and taught *Twenty Vows* and the extensive Hevajra sadhana to the astonishment of all, after his father passed away.

At thirteen, he received the three tantras of the Hevajra cycle in a dream, and comprehended the reality of all things. He also sponsored a great Dharma gathering in memory of his late father Sachen, and gave many teachings. The entire audience was amazed that he was able to recite the *Hevajra Root Tantra* from memory. Jetsun

Rinpoche continued his studies, practices and teachings in Sakya as commanded by his elder brother. Master Sonam Tsemo then departed to continue his studies at Sangphu in Central Tibet.

Jetsun Rinpoche was never separate from the samadhi of the two stages, creation and completion. When he went to give teaching he meditated Hevajra and when he settled on his throne, he concluded his practice up to the seal of the lord of his Buddha family. The general offerings represented the daily torma offerings. The Dharma teaching substituted for mantra repetitions. When he left to return to his residence he meditated Cakrasamvara. In this way, in one twenty four hour day, Jetsun Rinpoche meditated seventy individual deity mandalas.

As a sign of Jetsun Rinpoche's attainment, when the Kashmiri Pandita Shakya Shri-bhadra announced an eclipse of the Sun, because Jetsun Rinpoche performed a yogic practice, the eclipse did not occur. The Pandita said "To prove me wrong, Jetsun Rinpoche must have gone through every difficulty," and when the Pandita arrived to see Jetsun Rinpoche, Jetsun Rinpoche stood up suddenly, and left his vajra and bell hanging in space, etc. Because his signs of accomplishment were beyond comprehension, the Kashmiri Pandita Sakya Shri-bhadra praised Jetsun Rinpoche saying "Mahavajradhara Guhyasamaja!" and received the nectar of the teaching. Jetsun Rinpoche became the crown ornament of all the Arya Vajradharas.

At fifty six, Jetsun Rinpoche received the special instruction of the extremely close Path and Result lineage,

The Clear Meaning of Signs from the manifestation of Sachen's wisdom body at the Tsangkha monastery in Nyemo Rutsam at night in the state of clear light.

When Jetsun Rinpoche was sixty-eight and sixty-nine he blessed his own life to extend it by rejecting the invitations of the Dakinis from Sukhavati who came again and again.

Through explanation, debate and composition, Jetsun Rinpoche spread Buddhism, and in particular, he liberated many fortunate beings through the *Path and Result* teachings. In this way, Jetsun Rinpoche benefited limitless sentient being throughout his seventy years and passed in 1216 [fire rat year].

His main students were his nephews Sakya Pandita and Zangtsa. Further he had eight disciples with the last name 'Dragpa;' four disciples who held the teaching of *Vajrapanjara*. He had four great Vidyadhara disciples, and many others.

Jetsun Rinpoche himself predicted he would be reborn as the son of a Chakravartin King of the world 'Golden' where he was to accomplish most of the paths and stages, and at his third rebirth will become a Buddha.

Jetsun Rinpoche Dragpa Gyaltsen was fully conversant in all aspects of Buddhist learning, but for the most part his writings focused on the Vajrayana systems he received from his father and other teachers. These writings consist of commentaries on tantras, sadhanas, initiation, rituals, etc., from the Hevajra system, the Chakrasamavara system including Vajrayogini, and many others.

PRAISE OF THE TWENTY ONE TARAS

Translated by Tulku Thondup Rinpoche

In Indian (Sanskrit) language:
Aryataremantramulastrotranamaskaraikavimsatikanama

In Tibetan:
'Phags-Ma sGroi-Ma'i rTsa-Ba'i sNgags-Kyi bsTod-Ching
Phyag-'Tshal-Ba Nyi-Shu rTsa-gChig-Pa Zhes-Bya-Ba

OM JE-TSUN-MA PHAG-MA DROL-MA-LA CHAG-TSHAL LO
Om, I pay homage to the Revered Noble TARA (Savioress)

CHAG-TSHAL TA-RE NYUR-MA PA-MO
TUT-TA RA-YEE JIG-PA SEL-MA
TU-REE DON-KUN JIN-PE DROL-MA
SVA-HA YI-GE KHYOD-LA DUD-DO
Homage to TARA, swift and heroic,
TUTTARA, dispelling fear,
TURE, (swiftly) providing all the goals, Savioress,
And SVAHA letter, I bow to you.

OM JE-TSUN-MA PHAG-MA DROL-MA LA CHAG-TSHAL LO
CHAG-TSHAL DROL-MA NYUR-MA PA-MO
CHEN-NI KED-CHIG LOG-DANG DRA-MA
JIG-TEN SUM-GON CHU-KYEY ZHEL-GYI
GE-SAR CHE-WA LE-NI CHUNG-MA
Homage! TARA, swift, heroic
Whose eyes are instant like a lightning.
Who is born from the blossoming pistil of
The lotus face of the Lord of the Three Worlds.

CHAG-TSHAL TON-KA'I DA-WA KUN-TU
GANG-WA GYA-NI TSEG-PA'I ZHEL-MA
KAR-MA TONG-THRAG TSHOG-PA NAM-KYEE
RAB-TU CHE-WA'I OD-RAB BAR-MA
Homage! Whose face is a tier
Of the fullest hundred autumn moons.
Who is blazing with
Total resplendent light of a thousand stars.

CHAG-TSHAL SER-NGO CHU-NE KYEY-KYI
PAD-ME CHAG-NI NAM-PAR GYEN-MA
JIN-PA TSON-DROO KA-THUB ZHI-WA
ZOD-PA SAM-TEN CHOD-YUL NYID-MA
Homage! Who is golden and blue;
Her hand adorned with water-born lotuses.
Who enjoys giving, effort, calm,
Patience and contemplation.

CHAG-TSHAL DE-ZHIN SHEG-PA'I TSUG-TOR
THA-YE NAM-PAR GYAL-WAR CHOD-MA
MA-LOO PHA-ROL CHIN-PA THOB-PAI
GYAL-WAI SE-KYEE SHIN-TU TEN-MA
Homage! Who enjoys the crown-knot of Thus-Gones,
The infinite total victory;
Who is honoured by the Sons of the Conquerers,
Who have achieved the perfections.

CHAG-TSHAL TUT-TA RA-HUNG YI-GEE
DOD-DANG CHOG-DANG NAM-KHA GANG-MA
JIG-TEN DUN-PO ZHAB-KYEE NEN-TE
LOO-PA MED-PAR GUG-PAR NOO-MA
Homage! Who fills the regions, quarters and space
With TUTTARA HUM letters.
Who tramples the seven worlds with her feet and
Is able to summon all (beings).

CHAG-TSHAL GYA-JIN ME-LHA TSHANG-PA
LUNG-LHA NA-TSHOG WANG-CHUG CHOD-MA
JUNG-PO RO-LANG TRI-ZA NAM-DANG
NOD-JIN TSHOG-KYEE DUN-NE TOD-MA
Homage! Who is worshipped by Indra, Agni, Brahma,
Marut and Visvevara.
Who is praised, in her presence, by hosts of spirits,
Roving corpses, smell-eaters and Yaksas.

CHAG-TSHAL TRAD-CHEY CHA-DANG PHET-KYEE
PHA-ROL THRUL-KHOR RAB-DU JOM-MA
YE-KUM YON-KYANG ZHAB-KYEE NEN-TE
ME-BAR THRUG-PA SHIN-DU BAR-MA
Homage! Who is the destroyer of Mara's magic cycle
With sound of TRAD and PHAT
Who with eruption of blazing fire
Tramples with her right leg back and left leg extended.

CHAG-TSHAL TU-RE JIG-PA CHEN-MO
DUD-KYI PA-WO NAM-PAR JOM-MA
CHU-KYEY ZHEL-NI THRO-NYER DEN-DZED
DRA-WO THAM-CHED MA-LOO SOD-MA
Homage! Who is TURE, frightful,
Destroys the Mara's courage,
Who slays all the enemies
With the frown of her lotus face.

CHAG-TSHAL KON-CHOG SUM-TSHON CHAG-GYAI
SOR-MOO THUG-KAR NAM-PAR GYEN-MA
MA-LOO CHOG-GYI KHOR-LOO GYEN-PAI
RANG-GI OD-KYI TSHOG-NAM THRUG-MA
Homage! Who is adorned, at her heart
With her finger making the gesture of the Triple Jewel;
Who fills (all) with the mass of her light,
Adorning the wheel of all quarters (of the universe).

CHAG-TSHAL RAB-TU GA-WAR JID-PAI

U-GYEN OD-KYI THRENG-WA PEL-MA

ZHED-PA RAB-ZHED TUT-TA RA-YEE

DUD-DANG JIG-TEN WANG-TU DZED-MA

Homage! Who spreads garlands of lights of her crown
Which is majestic and joyful;
Who subjugates the world and Maras
With TUTTARE, laughing mirthfully.

CHAG-TSHAL SA-ZHI KYONG-WAI TSHOG-NAM

THAM-CHED GUG-PAR NOO-MA NYID-MA

THRO-NYER YO-WAI YI-GE HUNG-GEE

PHONG-PA THAM-CHED NAM-PAR DROL-MA

Homage! Who is able to summon
All the hosts of the lords of the earth;
Who protects from all the poverties
With waves of frown (wrath), the letter HUM.

CHAG-TSHAL DA-WAI DUM-BOO U-GYEN

GYEN-PA THAM-CHED SHIN-TU BAR-MA

RAL-PAI THROD-NE OD-PAG MED-LE

TAG-PAR SHIN-TU OD-RAB DZED-MA

Homage! Whose crown is adorned with a crescent moon
And who is totally blazing;
From her piled-up hair, Amitabha
Shines lights all the time.

CHAG-TSHAL KAL-WA THA-MAI ME-TAR
BAR-WA'I THRENG-WAI U-NA NE-MA
YE-KYANG YON-KUM KUN-NE KOR-GAI
DRA-YI PUNG-NI NAM-PAR JOM-MA
Homage! Who dwells amid a blazing ring
Which is like the fire at the end of the (world) era.
Her right leg extended and left leg back,
She destroys the enemy forces.

CHAG-TSHAL SA-ZHEE NGO-LA CHAG-GI
THIL-GYEE NUN-CHING ZHAB-KYEE DUNG-MA
THRO-NYER CHEN-DZED YI-GE HUNG-GEE
RIM-PA DUN-PO NAM-NI GEM-MA
Homage! Who strikes the earth with her palm
And pounds it with her feet;
Who shatters the seven underworlds,
Frowning, with the letter HUM.

CHAG-TSHAL DE-MA GE-MA ZHI-MA
NYA-NGEN DE-ZHI CHOD-YUL NYID-MA
SO-HA OM-DANG YANG-DAG DEN-PE
DIG-PA CHEN-PO JOM-PA NYID-MA
Homage! Who is blissful, virtuous and calm, and
Enjoys the peace of Nirvana.
Who destroys the awful unvirtuous deeds
By perfection of OM and (through) SVAHA.

CHAG-TSHAL KUN-NE KOR-RAB GA-WAI
DRA-YI LOO-NI RAB-TU GEM-MA
YI-GE CHU PAI NGAG-NI KOD PAI
RIG-PA HUNG-LE DROL-MA NYID-MA
Homage! Who encircles (protects) with joy and
Destroys the body of enemies.
Who protects with HUM science, and
The syllable-array of ten letters.

CHAG-TSHAL TU-REE ZHAB-NI DAB-PE
HUNG-GI NAM-PAI SA-BON NYID-MA
RI-RAB MEN-DA RA-DANG BIG-CHED
JIG-TEN SUM-NAM YO-WA NYID-MA
Homage! Who stamps her feet of TURE, and
Whose seed (-letter) is the form of HUM;
Who shakes Mt. Meru, Mandara, Vindhya
And the three worlds.

CHAG-TSHAL LHA-YI TSHO-YI NAM-PAI
RI-DAG TAG-CHEN CHAG-NA NAM-MA
TA-RA NYEE-JOD PHAT-KYI YI-GEE
DUG-NAM MA-LOO PA-NI SEL-MA
Homage! Who holds in her hand a deer-marked (moon),
Like "the lake of the gods;"
Who dispels the poison without remainder
With twice-uttered TARA and the PHAT letter.

CHAG TSHAL LHA-YI TSHOG-NAM GYAL-PO
LHA-DANG MI-AM CHI-YEE TEN-MA
KUN-NE GO-CHA GA-WAI JID-KYEE
TSOD-DANG MI-LAM NGEN-PA SEL-MA
Homage! Who is served by lord of hosts of gods,
Gods and Kinnaras;
Who dispels conflicts and bad dreams
With brilliance of joyous armor.

CHAG-TSHAL NYI-MA DA-WA GYE-PAI
CHEN-NYEE PO-LA OD-RAB SAL-MA
HA-RA NYEE-JOD TUT-TA RA-YEE
SHIN-DU TRAG-POI RIM-NED SEL-MA
Homage! From whose eyes rays are shining effulgently,
As (from) the sun and full moon;
Who drives out the terrible epidemics
With utterance of two HARAS and TUTARA.

CHAG-TSHAL DE-NYID SUM-NAM KOD-PE
ZHI-WAI THU-DANG YANG-DAG DEN-MA
DON-DANG RO-LANG NOD-JIN TSHOG-NAM
JOM-PA TUR-RE RAB-CHOG NYID-MA
Homage! Who, through the three aspects of suchness (syllables),
Perfectly endowed with the pacifying power;
Who is the supreme TURE, who destroys
The hosts of harmful spirits, roving corpses and Yaksas.

TSA-WAI NGAG-KYI TOD-PA DI-DANG
CHAG-TSHAL WA-NI NYI-SHU TSA-CHIG
This praise, rooted in mantras,
Has twenty-one sets of homages.

Note: According to Yum-Ka mKha'-Gro'i Nang-sGrub bDe-Chen sNying-Po'i gTer-Bum by Rigdzin Jigmed Lingpa, the names and benefits of the Twenty-One Taras are:

1. Nyurma Pamo (Myur-Ma dPa'-Mo) for development of the mind of enlightenment.
2. Yangchen-ma (dByangs-Chan-Ma, Skt., Sarasvati) for knowledge and wisdom.
3. Sodnam Chogter (bSod-Nams mCho'og-sTer) for the force of merit.
4. Tsugtor Namgyal (gTsug-Tor rNam-rGyal, Skt., Ushnisha-vijaya) for long life.
5. Rigched-ma (Rig-Byed-Ma, Skt., Kurukulli) for attracting and controlling people and wealth.
6. Jigched Chenmo ('Jigs-Byed Chen-Mo) for destruction of the power of harmful spirits.
7. Zhenyi Mithub-ma (gZhan-Gyi Mi-Thub-Ma) for protection from hailstorms and lightning.
8. Zhenmi Gyalwa (gZhan-Mi rGyal-Ba or gZhan Las rGyal) for repelling blame.
9. Sengdeng Nag-kyi Droma (Seng-lDeng Nags-Kyi sGrol-Ma, Skt., khadiravani-tara) for protection from eighteen great fears. She is the main Tara in green color.
10. Jigten Sumgyal ('Jigs-rTen gSum-rGyal) to have power over the world.
11. Norter-ma (Nor-sTer-Ma) for dispelling poverty and having good luck.
12. Tashi Donched (bKra-Shis Don-Byed) for having auspiciousness of children, fame, rain and so on.
13. Dapung Jomma (dGra-dPung 'Joms-Ma) for victory in war.
14. Thro-nyer Chen-dzed (Khro-gNyer Chan-mDzed, Skt., Bhrkuti) for protection from spirit forces.
15. Rabtu Zhiwa (Rab-Tu Zhi-Ba) for purifying evil deeds.
16. Barwa'i Odchen ('Bar-Wa'i A'od-Chan) for dispelling spells and negative effects.
17. Pagmed Nonma (dPag-Med gNon-Ma) for protection from robbers, thieves, animals and hunters.
18. Macha Chenmo (rMa-Bya Chen-Mo) to protect from and neutralize poisons.
19. Mipham Gyalmo (Mi-Pham rGyal-Mo) for protection from quarrels and bad dreams.

20. Rithrod-ma (Ri-Khrod-Ma) for protection from epidemics.
21. Odzer Chenma (A'od-Zer Chan-Ma) for restoring the spirits and energies of sick people.

Manjushri Press began as Prajna Press in India where it published important Buddhist texts in Tibetan. It has since been reorganized as Manjushri Press and now publishes books in English about Buddhism and Tibet. For more information about our projects, please contact:

Manjushri Press
P.O. Box 391042
Cambridge, Massachusetts 02139
USA
phone/fax: (617) 492-2614
e-mail: MANJUSHRI@earthlink.net